G.E. WOODAGE

JACK THE RIPPER
BEYOND THE GRAVE

THE LIFE AND CRIMES OF
CHARLES ALLEN LECHMERE

This edition first published in paperback by
Michael Terence Publishing in 2024
www.mtp.agency

Copyright © 2024 G.E. Woodage

G.E. Woodage has asserted the right to be identified as
the author of this work in accordance with the
Copyright, Designs and Patents Act 1988

ISBN 9781800947856

No part of this publication may be reproduced, stored
in a retrieval system, or transmitted, in any form or
by any means, electronic, mechanical, photocopying,
recording or otherwise, without the prior
permission of the publisher

Cover design
Copyright © 2024 Michael Terence Publishing

Michael Terence
Publishing

Contents

1: A Picture of the Victorian East End 1
2: My Name is Lechmere 4
3: Martha Tabram – from Beyond the Grave 12
4: Charles Lechmere – from Beyond the Grave 15
5: Polly Nichols – from Beyond the Grave 25
6: I Meet With an Angel 28
7: Annie Chapman – from Beyond the Grave 33
8: Charles Allen Lechmere – from Beyond the Grave 36
9: Elizabeth Stride – from Beyond the Grave 39
10 Charles Allen Lechmere – from Beyond the Grave 42
11: Catherine Eddowes – from Beyond the Grave 46
12: I Meet With a Devil 49
13: Mary Jane Kelly – from Beyond the Grave 52
14: Murder – But Not By My Hands 56
15: The Murder of Martha Tabram 62
16: Inspector Edmund Reid – from Beyond the Grave 66
17: The Angel of Death 69
18: Frederick Abberline – from Beyond the Grave 74
19: The Inquest of Polly Nichols 80
21: Charles Allen Lechmere – from Beyond the Grave.
 The Murder of Annie Chapman 88

22: Edward Swanson – from Beyond the Grave 90

23: Charles Allen Lechmere – from Beyond the Grave.
The Double Event 94

24 Frederick Abberline – from Beyond the Grave 99

25: Charles Allen Lechmere – from Beyond the Grave.
The Bloody Cloth 105

26: George Lusk – from Beyond the Grave. From Hell 107

27: Charles Allen Lechmere – from Beyond the Grave.
The Murder of Mary Jane Kelly 110

28: Frederick Abberline – from Beyond the Grave.
Senseless Murder 114

29: Lechmere – The Butcher of Whitechapel 120

30: Donald Swanson – from Beyond the Grave 124

31: Charles Lechmere – from Beyond the Grave 132

1
A Picture of the Victorian East End

The streets of Victorian London's East End were a sight to behold. Crowded and bustling, they were a melting pot of people from all walks of life. But amidst the energy and chaos, there was a sense of despair and hopelessness that hung thick in the air.

The people of the East End were a hardworking and resilient lot. They toiled day and night, doing whatever they could to scrape together a meager existence. But try as they might, they could never escape the poverty and misery that seemed to be their constant companion.

One of the most notorious aspects of the East End was the squalor. The tenements were overcrowded and dilapidated, with families squeezed into tiny rooms, living in squalid conditions. The streets were littered with garbage and waste, and there was a constant stench of human excrement and decay.

The pubs of the East End were a popular haunt for the working class. Here, they could escape the harsh realities of their lives and drown their sorrows in cheap alcohol. But the pubs were also a breeding ground for violence and debauchery. Drunken brawls were a common occurrence, and it was not uncommon to see men staggering out of the establishments, clutching onto a bottle of gin for dear life.

And speaking of gin, it was in the East End that the illegal production of the spirit thrived. Backstreet stills were hidden away in dark alleyways, churning out gallons of the potent drink. And in the pubs, the sale of illegal gin was rampant, with the owners turning a blind eye to the law in order to make a quick profit.

The drinking habits of the poor were a cause for concern. Many turned to alcohol as a means of coping with their harsh reality, and it was not uncommon to see young children drinking alongside their parents. In fact, alcoholism was so prevalent in the East End that it was estimated that one in every three households had at least one family member who struggled with addiction.

Prostitution was another dark underbelly of the East End. Women turned to this profession as a means of survival, selling their bodies for a few measly coins. And it was not just women who were involved in this trade. Child prostitution was also rampant, with young boys and girls being forced into this dangerous and degrading profession by people who saw them as little more than commodities.

Cottaging, a term used to describe the practice of men soliciting sex with young boys, was also shockingly prevalent in the East End. These boys, often from poor and vulnerable backgrounds, were lured in with promises of money and a better life, only to be subjected to unspeakable abuse by their clients.

But perhaps the most disturbing aspect of the East End was the trade of young virgins. Men with twisted desires would pay exorbitant amounts of money to a pimp who would procure a young virgin for them. These girls, some as young as 13 or 14, were then sold to these men for their vile purposes. And the most heartbreaking part was that some parents, desperate for money, would willingly hand over their daughters to these pimps, not realizing the fate that awaited their innocent children.

Along with all these social issues, the East End was also plagued by civil unrest. The poor were tired of living in squalor and being subjected to injustices and exploitation. And as a result, riots and demonstrations were a common occurrence, with the people demanding better living conditions and fair treatment.

The streets of the East End were also a haven for pickpockets, muggers, and burglars. With so many impoverished and vulnerable people, it was easy for these criminals to find easy targets. And in a place where survival was a daily struggle, many were willing to resort to any means necessary to get by.

Venereal disease was another scourge of the East End. With prostitution and promiscuity at an all-time high, diseases such as syphilis and gonorrhea were rampant, spreading easily from person to person. And with little to no access to proper medical care, these diseases often led to painful and untimely deaths.

As one can imagine, the streets of Victorian London's East End were not for the faint-hearted. They were filled with despair, exploitation, and danger at every turn. And for the poor souls who called this place home, every day was a struggle to survive in a world that seemed to have no place for them.

And little did these poor people of the East End know, that something would cast an even darker shadow upon the dark squalid streets of Whitechapel in 1888. Many a woman feared to go out at night, all feared something much more dangerous than poverty. A demon walked the streets, praying upon the prostitutes of the city. And that demon came to be known as JACK THE RIPPER.

2
My Name is Lechmere

My name is Charles Allen Lechmere, but most people just called me Charlie. And I speak to you from beyond the grave. I was born in the East End of London on a rainy night in 1849. My parents were John Allen Lechmere and Maria Louisa Lechmere. My father was a bootmaker with a small shop in the East End, and my mother... well, let's just say she was quite a character.

My mother was a very domineering woman, always barking orders and never taking no for an answer. She was strict, oh so strict, and she made sure her children knew it. My sister Emily Charlotte was two years older than me, and she and I were often at the receiving end of my mother's discipline. We were never allowed to speak out of turn or even play too loudly. Mother believed in raising her children with a firm hand and quick to use her trusty cane if we stepped out of line.

But it wasn't just us children that suffered under my mother's strict rules. She also nagged my father endlessly, never satisfied with the way he ran his boot making business. My father was a kind and gentle man, but after some time, he couldn't take my mother's nagging anymore. He left her and us children behind, taking whatever money he had with him, and moved to Daventry to start a new life. My mother's drinking didn't help matters either.

I was only four years old when my father left, so I have very few memories of him other than what my uncle Sid tells me. Uncle Sid is my father's brother and works in a slaughterhouse in Winthrop Street. I've always been drawn to his job, fascinated by the skill and strength it takes to handle those big, powerful creatures. But my mother was adamantly against it. She believed it was a dirty and sinful job, and she wouldn't have her children associating with such work.

Mother was also very religious, and we were expected to attend church every Sunday. I remember sitting through the vicar's sermons, filled with fire and brimstone, talking about the sins of the flesh and fallen women. I couldn't help but wonder if my father had left us because my mother had committed some terrible sin that angered God.

But life went on, and we had to make ends meet. Without a father to provide for our family, my sister and I had to find ways to earn money. I took on odd jobs, running errands for the neighbors, while Emily worked as a seamstress. It wasn't easy, but we managed to get by.

One day, I begged my mother to let me visit Uncle Sid at the slaughterhouse. I had heard rumors that it was a gruesome and bloody place, but something inside of me was drawn to it. My mother, of course, refused, but with a bit of pleading and some exaggerated promises to behave, she finally gave in.

As soon as I stepped into the slaughterhouse, I was hit with the smells and sounds. The smell of blood and death hung heavy in the air, and the constant mooing of the cattle echoed throughout the building. It was overwhelming at first, but I quickly got used to it.

I watched in awe as Uncle Sid and his workers skillfully killed and prepared the animals for butchering. I couldn't help but ask my uncle why there wasn't much blood on him, even though he was slaughtering cattle all day. He chuckled and told me that once the animal's heart stopped, once the creature is dead, you get no spray of blood,' he said matter-of-factly.

That statement stuck with me, and I couldn't stop thinking about it. Uncle Sid's explanation made perfect sense to me, and I couldn't wait to share it with my mother. Maybe if she understood that a man could work in such a place without being covered in blood and filth, she would let me find work with uncle Sid as a slaughterman.

But as I grew older, I realized that it wasn't just the job that my mother didn't approve of. It was the lifestyle, the people. Uncle Sid and his colleagues were rough and uncouth, speaking in a thick cockney accent that my mother found repulsive. I, on the other hand, found it endearing and familiar.

I often found myself longing for that life, working alongside my uncle and his fellow butchers. But my mother's strict rules kept me in check, reminding me that I was meant for a more respectable job. I was only eleven years old, and despite my inner desires, I took on a job as a carman's assistant, delivering meat from the Pickford's Depot, which was located near Broad Street goods yard, to different businesses and homes around London. It wasn't easy work, but it paid the bills. I worked from Monday to Saturday, from four thirty am, and worked throughout the day in all weathers, until we had finished delivering our last load, which sometimes wasn't till late evening. I had very little time that I could call my own.

Growing up in Victorian London's East End was not an easy life. As a carter's assistant, my days were filled with long hours of hard labour. But on my one day off, I always made time to visit the Whitechapel Road market. It was a bustling and lively place, filled with the sounds of different languages and the chants of the market sellers.

As I made my way through the crowded streets, I could hear the familiar cries of the sellers as they called out their wares.

'Fresh fruits and vegetables! Get em while they're ripe!'

'Fine clothes for a penny! Don't miss ya chance, ladies and gents!'

The market was a feast for the senses. The smell of freshly baked bread and roasted meat mixed with the vibrant colors of the stalls. There were all kinds of goods being sold, from food and clothing to antiques and trinkets. It was a place where you could find almost anything, if you looked hard enough.

But amidst the chaos and commotion, there were also dangers lurking. Pickpockets were known to target unsuspecting customers, and children would sometimes steal from the stalls when the sellers were not looking. It was a harsh reality of life in the East End, where poverty was rampant and survival was a daily struggle.

On one particular day at the market, as I was browsing the stalls, I noticed my thirteen-year-old sister Emily talking to a well-known prostitute and seller of child prostitution, Martha Tabram. My heart sank as I saw the two of them huddled together, their faces serious as they spoke. Knowing the type of person Martha was, I made my way through the crowd and stood hidden, so I could hear what was being said.

Martha asked Emily if she was a virgin, to which Emily did not answer. My heart raced with fear and anger as I listened on. I knew that Martha was trying to recruit my sister into prostitution, and I had to do something to stop it.

As Martha continued to speak, my blood boiled with rage. 'Have you ever been with a man?' she asked Emily once more.

'No,' replied Emily, her voice barely above a whisper.

Martha's next words pierced through my heart like a knife. 'Would you like to earn two bob for ten minutes' work?'

Without hesitation, Emily replied, 'Yes.'

My heart ached with sadness and anger as I watched my sister fall for Martha's manipulative words, for I knew that a rich toff would pay Martha about five pounds for a fresh innocent virgin like my sister, that way they knew there was no chance of picking up a dose of the clap.

Then pointing to a corner of the street, Martha said. Be a good girl and go with that toff who is standing over there on the corner, and I'll pay you when you come back.

Tears welled up in my eyes as I watched Emily walk towards the man, her innocence about to be taken away. But I couldn't just stand by and let it happen. I rushed towards them, my heart pounding in my chest.

When I reached the man, I was filled with fear and anger. He was much taller and stronger than me, but I couldn't let him hurt my sister. I kicked him in the shins, causing him to stumble in surprise.

'You filthy bastard!' I shouted at him, my anger bubbling over. 'Leave my sister alone!' The man glared at me, his hand raised as if to strike me. But before he could do anything, I heard a commotion behind me. It was the market sellers, who had come to see what all the shouting was about.

One of the sellers, a burly man with a kind heart, recognized me as the carter's assistant and quickly came to my aid. Together, we managed to chase off the man and protect my sister from his clutches.

But my anger towards Martha was still burning strong. I called her a filthy whore and vowed to pay her back when I had grown older. It was the only thing I could do at that moment, as I was still just a young boy with little power.

As we made our way back home, my sister and I talked about what had transpired at the market. I explained to her the dangers of prostitution and how Martha's words were nothing but lies. Emily was scared, but she understood now and promised to never trust anyone ever again.

As we approached our house, we stopped, and I wiped the tears from Emily's eyes, and told her not to say a word to Mother. Emily promised that she wouldn't say a word, and I saw her safely to the front door, and waited until she was safely inside.

My anger and hatred of that filthy whore Martha Tabram, was still with me as I made my way down the street and into a deserted stable yard. Sitting upon an old wooden box, I thought of how I could deal with that whore black Martha.

As I sat in the deserted stable yard in Bucks Row, my thoughts were consumed with anger and hatred. The wooden box beneath me creaked as I shifted my weight, lost in my dark musings.

Martha Tabram, the name alone made my blood boil. The filthy whore had dared to approach my innocent sister, trying to tempt her into a life of prostitution. The thought of Martha preying on young, vulnerable girls ignited a fire within me. I had caught wind of her despicable actions and had been boiling with rage ever since.

But what could I do? I was just a young boy, barely old enough to be considered a man. I had no power, no voice. And even if I did speak out, who would listen? The police were known to turn a blind eye to the unfortunate souls of the East End. I had seen it happen countless times. The poor were left to fend for themselves while the rich looked down upon us with disdain.

My anger grew with every passing moment, fueling my hatred towards all those women of the night, all those vile prostitutes. They were the reason for the degradation of our society, preying on men's weaknesses and leading them down a path of destruction.

I sat there, my anger boiling over, when suddenly a cat appeared in the stable yard. It sauntered towards me, its eyes glowing in the dim light, and began to rub itself against my legs. I pushed it away, but it kept coming back, persistent in its attempts to gain my attention.

My anger reached a peak as the cat's meows filled the quiet yard. Without a second thought, I grabbed the creature by its neck and started to strangle it. It struggled and clawed at my arms, drawing blood, but I didn't falter. I kept on throttling it, my anger giving me strength, until the life faded from its eyes and its body went limp in my hands.

Looking down at the dead cat, I felt a sense of satisfaction wash over me. Its lifeless body lay in my hands, a small victory against the evil that plagued our streets.

In a trance-like state, I retrieved my knife from my pocket and began to mutilate the cat's body. I relished in the sight of its blood oozing out onto the ground, a small puddle forming at my feet. It was then that the thought struck me - what if I did the same to that filthy whore Martha Tabram?

But no, I told myself. Not yet. I was still young, and my plans needed time to come to fruition. I couldn't risk getting caught and ruining my plans for revenge. No, I needed to bide my time and wait for the perfect opportunity to present itself.

With that thought, I disposed of the cat's body in the mud and made my way back home. My mind was consumed with the dark thoughts, the gruesome details of how I would exact my revenge on Martha Tabram the filthy whore.

It was a chilly Monday morning in Victorian London's bustling East End. After a Sunday of rest, I returned to my work as a Carman's assistant. After many deliveries throughout that chilly day, the great shire horse that pulled our cart, made its way down the busy streets with a heavy clip clop. I was going to help old Tommy Parker deliver the last load of meat to the meat processors on Winthrop Street.

As we made our way through the crowded streets, I couldn't help but notice the stench of the nearby slaughterhouse where my uncle Sid worked. And as we passed its gates, my uncle suddenly appeared before us, a look of concern on his face.

He told me about a young friend of mine, called Tiny Johnson, who had been attacked and left for dead. My heart sank at the thought of seeing such violence in our already rough neighborhood.

Curious and worried, I asked my uncle where Tiny had been taken. His answer made my stomach turn - a hospital for the poor, just off the Whitechapel Road. Without a second thought, I asked Tommy if it was okay for me to go and check on my friend. He assured me that we were almost done with our delivery and he could handle the remaining load on his own.

So I ran down the filthy streets, dodging people and horse-drawn carriages, until I reached the rundown hospital. The conditions were worse than I could have imagined - dirty, dimly-lit rooms filled with the sick and injured. Flies crawled over some of the patients' open wounds, making my skin crawl.

I asked a nurse, if you could call her that, about my friend and was met with a stench of alcohol on her breath and a look of indifference on her face. Her clothes were filthy and I couldn't help but think that Tiny would have been better off without her care.

Finally, after what felt like an eternity, I found my friend lying on an old mattress in a damp corner of the room. He looked so weak and frail, it broke my heart. I asked him who had done this to him and he whispered the names of two women - Emma Smith and Fairy Fay.

According to Tiny, he had been forced into being a cottaging boy by the two women. One day, he went to an alley with a well-to-do gentleman and after the man had had his way with him, he refused to pay. Fearful of what Emma and Fairy would do if he returned with no money, Tiny begged the man to give him what he was owed. But the man only looked around to make sure no one was watching and then brutally beat Tiny with his silver-tipped cane, leaving him in a pool of blood.

As Tiny finished his story, his eyes closed and he took his last breath. My heart shattered at that moment and I made a mental note of Emma and Fairy's names, vowing to avenge Little Tiny's death.

I added their names to my ever-growing list of people who had wronged me or the people in my community, and I swore to make them pay for what they had done to my dear friend. This was just another cruel reminder of the harsh reality of life in the East End, where violence and injustice seemed to be a daily occurrence.

3
Martha Tabram
– from Beyond the Grave

I was born in the Victorian East End of London on 10th May 1849. My name is Martha Tabram and I speak to you now from beyond the grave. My story is not one of glamor and riches, but rather one of hardship and desperation.

My parents were simple Londoners, working hard to make ends meet. I was the youngest of four children and often felt overlooked in the hustle and bustle of our home. Despite this, I was always a happy child, finding joy in the simplest things.

I was married to my husband, Henry Tabram, in 1869 and we were blessed with two beautiful children. But our marriage was short-lived, as my husband left me after just four years. He worked at the London Docks and I suppose my liking of the bottle, and the long hours and physical labour took its toll on him. He left, taking our children with him, and I never set eyes upon them again.

With my husband gone and my children taken from me, I felt lost and alone. Desperate to make ends meet, I went from job to job. But I soon discovered that I had a problem with stealing. Things would always seem to go missing at my places of work and I would inevitably be let go.

The money I did earn was just enough to pay for the tiny, dirty room where I lived. But soon, my drinking became worse and I spent every penny I had on gin. Eventually, I was thrown out onto the streets, with nowhere to go.

That's when I met an old friend, Fairy Fay. She was also struggling to make ends meet and offered me a place to stay in her room. She told me that she had turned to prostitution to survive and suggested that I do the same if I wanted to stay under her roof and eat.

At first, I was hesitant, but as days went by and my desperation deepened, I gave in and became a prostitute. It was easy work and I soon found myself in the company of other women like me. The only problem was that Fairy Fay and I were both heavy drinkers and often spent our profits on cheap gin at the nearest pub.

One of our regular haunts was the Ten Bells pub. It was a dingy and crowded place, filled with the smell of sweat and alcohol, and the air thick with smoke. The atmosphere was chaotic, with drunken men shouting and laughing, and women trying to catch their attention.

Fairy Fay and I would sit in the corner, nursing our two half pints of gin and discussing our plans to earn more money. That's when Fay came up with a sinister idea - to start a trade in child prostitution.

She explained that there was a demand for young boys for 'cottaging' and young virgin girls for the pleasure of wealthy men. The men would pay handsomely for the use of these children, offering up to five pounds for a virgin. And we would only have to give a small portion of that money to the children, while pocketing the rest for ourselves.

At first, I was horrified and wanted nothing to do with such a despicable act. But Fairy Fay was persuasive and eventually, I agreed to her plan.

We left the pub that night, determined to find innocent and unsuspecting children who we could exploit for our own gain. And we succeeded in our sickening quest, never getting caught but earning a substantial amount of money, most of which went on gin.

But eventually, karma caught up with me. In 1888, I was found dead upon the first floor landing of George Yard Buildings, with

39 stab wounds on my body. My gruesome murder sent shockwaves through the Victorian East End. I was the first victim of Jack the Ripper.

As I look back on my life now, I can't help but feel remorse for my actions. I paid the ultimate price for my greed and desperation. But I hope that my story serves as a warning to others, to not let desperation and greed cloud their judgment. For it can lead to a tragic and untimely end, just like it did for me.

4
Charles Lechmere
– from Beyond the Grave

My name is Charles Allen Lechmere, and I speak to you from beyond the grave.

Not long after little Tiny Johnson's death, I saw a change in my mother. She had stopped drinking, and our house was regularly visited by a police constable by the name of Thomas Cross. He was a big, good-hearted man, and always had a smile for anyone he met. I liked him straight away, and so did my older sister Emily.

He would drop in for a cup of tea when he was on his beat, or for something a little stronger if he was off duty. Over time, his visits became more regular, and my mother seemed to like him very much. I was now thirteen years old, and Emily was fifteen. A few months after their first meeting, my mother announced that Thomas and she were to be married.

But there was a problem. We didn't know if my father, who had left us when I was just four years old, was alive or dead. My mother told us to keep the marriage a secret, for it would be bigamous if my father was still alive. So on the day of the wedding in 1858, we all traveled away from our local area, and to a church in the west end of London.

The ceremony was small, with only Emily and I in the congregation. It was a bittersweet moment, for though I was happy for my mother, I couldn't help but feel a pang of sadness knowing that my father was not with us anymore.

With their marriage official, Thomas became a permanent fixture in our little family. It was a relief for me, as I was no longer the man of the household. But I was also intrigued by Thomas's profession. He was a police constable in H Division, patrolling the streets of Whitechapel. I would often ask him about his job, and he would share stories of his encounters with the rough inhabitants of London's East End.

As I got to know Thomas more, I also learned that he was a kind and compassionate man. He would often take me and my sister out on walks around the city, showing us the sights and sounds of Victorian London. I cherished those moments, for they were the only happy memories I had of my childhood.

But there was one aspect of Thomas's job that intrigued me the most - his nightly patrols. My mother would often send me out at night to give my stepfather some sandwiches and a little something to warm him up. It was during these nightly errands that I would accompany Thomas on his beat, walking closely with him as he patrolled the streets.

I learned the times that the local bobbies would be at different locations, and made a mental note of it all. It was like a game to me, and I found myself becoming quite good at it. I knew the streets and the people that roamed them like the back of my hand.

As I grew older, my stepfather became like a mentor to me. He taught me the importance of being a good and just man, and I admired him greatly.

As a young boy growing up in 1800s London, I never would have imagined the life that lay ahead of me. My family lived in the bustling city, in the heart of the East End. We were not wealthy by any means, but we were happy. My stepfather, a police officer, provided a steady income, while my mother had started her own business selling cat's meat. My sister Emily was a skilled seamstress and also contributed to our household income. And I myself worked as a carter's assistant for the Pickford's Depot at Broad Street.

As the years went by, we found ourselves living fairly comfortably. With the combined money from our various jobs, we were able to afford a small but cozy home and even save a little for the future. It was a far cry from the poverty that many families in the East End experienced.

I enjoyed my work as a carter's assistant, as it allowed me to see different parts of the city and interact with a variety of people. And my stepfather always reminded me how fortunate I was to have a job, as many young boys my age were forced into factory work or other labour-intensive jobs, or even crime, which many had to do just to survive.

But everything changed when I turned eighteen. I had grown into a strong young man, and was very muscular for my age. One day, the manager of the Pickford's Depot at Broad Street called me to his office. My heart raced as I wondered what I could have possibly done wrong to warrant a summons from the manager.

As I nervously entered the office, the manager greeted me with a warm smile and asked me to take a seat. He then surprised me by asking how I would like to become a carter with my own horse and cart. It took a moment for his words to sink in, but when they did, I couldn't contain my excitement.

I stammered out a 'yes, please' and thanked the manager profusely for the opportunity. He then explained that I would have to come in earlier than my usual work hours, as I would now have to take care of my own horse and cart. But I didn't mind one bit.

With my head held high and a burst of newfound confidence, I made my way to the stables to meet my new horse and companion. And there he was, the magnificent Goliath. He was a massive shire horse, with a glossy coat that shone in the sunlight. He had a small white splash on his forehead, and as I approached him, he snorted and pawed at the ground, almost as if he was eager to meet me.

My foreman, Tom, welcomed me with a wide grin and said, 'Well, now you're a fully-fledged Pickford's carman, Charlie my lad. But it also means you'll have to start earlier, to harness

Goliath and prepare your cart for the day's work. Are you ready for the responsibility?'

I couldn't stop smiling as I replied, 'Yes, sir. I am ready.'

And with that, my journey as a carter officially began. I quickly learned how to take care of Goliath, from grooming and feeding him to harnessing him to the cart effortlessly. He was like a gentle giant, and we formed an immediate bond. We were a team, and I was determined to take good care of him.

As we began our daily routine, I couldn't help but feel a sense of pride and fulfillment in my new job. I was no longer just an assistant; I was now a carter, responsible for delivering meat all around London.

The days were long and physically demanding, but I loved every moment of it. I got to see parts of London that I never knew existed, from the grand mansions of the wealthy to the small shops and businesses of the working class. And Goliath was my companion throughout it all, his powerful hooves steadily carrying us from one location to another.

But as much as I enjoyed my new job, there were also dangers lurking in the streets of 1800s London. Thieves and robbers were a constant threat, and I had to keep a sharp eye out for anyone trying to steal my cargo. But with Goliath by my side, I felt safe and protected.

As the years went by, I became a well-respected carter in the Pickford's company. I was known for my hard work and dedication. My family, too, had done well, and we were no longer struggling to make ends meet.

Looking back on those early days, I am grateful for the opportunity that was given to me. A chance to become a carter, to have my own horse and cart, and to see the world in a different way. I never thought that a simple job could bring me so much joy and fulfillment.

As the years went by, I found that the people of the East End respected me. They even took to giving me friendly nicknames like 'good old Charlie' or 'Charlie boy'. It was a sign that I had been accepted into their community, and I couldn't be more proud.

You see, I've always been a hard worker. I may not have been the strongest or fastest carter, but I made up for it with hard work and honesty. People could count on me to deliver their goods on time and in perfect condition. This earned me a reputation as a reliable and trustworthy man.

But there was something else about me that the people of the East End didn't know. I had a darker side, a side that I kept hidden from the world. It was a side that only emerged when I was alone, or when I heard the voices in my head. I've heard these voices, whispering terrible things to me. At first, I thought I was going mad. But as I grew older, I realized that they were a part of me, a part that I couldn't ignore.

The voices would often speak of vengeance. They would tell me to seek revenge on those who wronged me, who hurt me and my friends and family. And the one that fueled my rage the most, were the voices that spoke of the prostitutes in the East End. They would tell me how these women had ruined the lives of the people I loved, and how they were all to blame for my misery. And it wasn't just the voices, but the memories of my past that haunted me.

The memories of my beloved sister, who was taken advantage of by one of those women.

I know it may sound strange, but the voices felt like a part of me. They were my constant companions, always urging me to act on my rage. And sometimes, in moments of weakness, I would listen.

But while the people of the East End saw me as a kind and cheerful man, the voices in my head knew the truth. They knew how I harbored an inner darkness, a hatred that burned deep within me. But I found I could push the voices away for a time.

That part of me that longed for violence, and revenge could wait a few years longer, then I would put terror into the hearts of those filthy whores.

As I went about my daily routine, delivering goods and chatting freely with the people I met on the streets, the voices grew louder. They whispered in my ear, reminding me of my mission, of the justice that needed to be served.

But I knew that I couldn't act on my impulses. I couldn't let the darkness take over me. So, I tried my best to suppress the voices, to ignore their demands. It wasn't easy, but I managed to keep them at bay for the most part.

However, there were times when I simply couldn't hold back. Like on one particular night, when I came across a group of prostitutes in a dimly lit alley. The voices in my head were screaming, urging me to take action. And despite my efforts to resist, I couldn't fight the urge any longer. I lunged at the women, driven by a primal desire for vengeance. Fortunately, I was able to snap out of it before I caused any harm. But the experience left me drained and terrified of the monster that lurked within me.

This war within myself continued for years. And while the people of the East End saw me as a friendly and jovial man, I struggled with the darkness that threatened to consume me. But deep down, I knew that I couldn't escape my past, that I would always be haunted by the injustice that had been done to my family and friends.

It was a morning in July 1869, and I remember it like it was yesterday. I woke up at my usual time of three am to get ready for a long day of work. As I got out of bed, I noticed that my mother was already up and in the little kitchen, boiling a kettle. I asked her why she was up at such an early hour and what she was doing.

My mother explained that my sister Emily had come down with a nasty cold and she was making her some hot honey and lemon to try and ease her symptoms. Even though my mother was not a woman who showed her love with affection, I could see the worry in her eyes. It was clear that she was concerned about Emily's health.

After making me a cup of tea and putting my boxes of sandwiches on the table, my mother kissed me on the forehead and went upstairs to tend to Emily. I quickly made my breakfast and washed up before leaving our small house at around three thirty am. The walk to my workplace at Pickford's Broad Street took about forty minutes, but I didn't mind the long journey. I was grateful to have a job, even if it meant starting work before the sun rose.

I worked throughout the hot day, transporting meat for Pickford's. The work was exhausting, but I was used to it. I didn't return home until seven pm, and when I walked into the little kitchen, I could see a worried look on my mother's face. She told me that my sister's condition had worsened since I left in the morning. The doctor had been called and had attended to Emily. He told us that she had consumption and there was nothing more that he could do.

I couldn't believe it. My sister, the sweet and kind Emily, was slowly slipping away from us. I felt a knot form in my stomach and tears prick at my eyes. A week later, Emily passed away.

As we gathered for her funeral, I couldn't help but think about Martha Tabram, and Fairy Faye.

Martha was a prostitute who had tried to steal Emily's innocence when she was just a young girl. I had caught her and rescued Emily away before she could do any harm, but the incident had left a deep scar on Emily. I remembered the way my sister had cried and how she had refused to leave the house for days after that.

And now, here we were, mourning her death. I could hear the voices in my head, calling for vengeance upon Martha Tabram, and Fairy Fay. I realized that I couldn't let her get away with what she had done to my dear sister. I made a vow to myself that I would make sure that the streets of Whitechapel were no longer safe for prostitutes like Martha Tabram.

In the year of 1869, a dark cloud of sorrow loomed over our household. It was a year that marked the loss of two beloved members of our family. My dear sister and my stepfather, who had been a light in my life for the short time he was married to my mother.

My mother had brought my sister and I up, being both mother and father to us for many years before she met Thomas. My birth father having left the family when I was only four years old. Leaving her to raise my sister and I on her own. But when Thomas came into our lives, he brought a newfound sense of love and stability. He treated my sister and me as if we were his own children, and we adored him for that.

It all started when Thomas began complaining of pains in his chest. My mother, being the caring woman she was, immediately called for the doctor. Dr. Roberts diagnosed him with a heart condition and advised that he should retire from his job as a policeman. We were all stunned by the news, especially my stepfather.

He never believed that his condition was as serious as the doctor had made it out to be. He was a strong man, both physically and mentally, and he refused to give up his job. He believed that he still had many years of service left in him.

However, as weeks went by, Thomas's health began to deteriorate rapidly. He started experiencing swelling of the skin, and my mother became increasingly worried. She called for the doctor once more, but my stepfather remained adamant that he was fine. He didn't want to believe that his body was failing him.

But soon enough, it became clear that he was not well. He was bedridden, and my mother had to take care of him while still trying to manage our household. I had to take on more responsibility at just twenty years of age. It was a difficult time for all of us.

The doctor was called once more, and this time, he told my mother that my stepfather had a condition called dropsy. It was a disease that caused excess fluid to build up in the body, and unfortunately, there was no cure. My mother and I were devastated, but we tried our best to make my stepfather as comfortable as possible.

It was a heartbreaking sight to see him suffer, and within a week, he passed away. My mother and I were left to mourn his loss, but we also had to think about our future. With my stepfather gone, I became the man of the house, and I had to step up and take care of my mother.

The day of the funeral was a somber one. We buried my stepfather in Tower Hamlets cemetery, a large and peaceful place, which was further over in the East End of London. The weather that day reflected our mood - gloomy and rainy. The only people present were the vicar, my mother, my uncle Sid, and myself.

My uncle Sid had come out of respect for my stepfather, and I was grateful for his presence. It was a small gathering, but I knew that my stepfather would have appreciated the simple and quiet send-off.

As we laid my stepfather to rest, memories flooded my mind. Memories of his gentle smile, his protective nature, and his unwavering love for my mother and me. I knew that he would be sorely missed, but I also knew that he would always be with us in spirit.

After the funeral, life went on, but it was never the same. My mother and I had to adjust to a new way of living. I had to work harder to provide for our small family, and my mother carried on with her cats meat business, which as the years passed became quite profitable. We relied on each other for support, and together, we managed to get through those tough times.

Now, many years later, I look back from the grave upon that year of 1869 with a heavy heart. It was a year that took two precious souls away from me, but it was also a year that taught me the importance of family and the strength we can find in each other during difficult times. And although I lost my dear stepfather, the memories of his kindness and love live on in my heart forever.

5

Polly Nichols

– from Beyond the Grave

My name is Mary Ann Nichols, but most people call me Polly. And I speak to you now, from beyond the grave. My story begins on the 26th of August, 1845, the day I entered this world in Dean Street, off Fetter Lane in London's East End. My parents, Edward and Caroline Walker, were hardworking, but they struggled to provide for our family. I was the second of three children, and we lived in a small cramped room in a rundown tenement. I won't bore you with the details of my childhood, for it was a difficult and unhappy time.

At the age of eighteen, I married a printers' machinist named William Nichols. We exchanged vows on the 16th of January, 1864 at St. Bride's Parish Church in the city of London. For a short time, we rented rooms at 30, 31 Bouverie Street, but soon realized we couldn't afford the rent. We moved in with my father at 131 Trafalgar Square.

Over the next thirteen years, we had five children, but our marriage was strained due to my excessive drinking.

In September 1879, we moved into our own home at 6 Peabody Buildings. We paid a weekly rent of five shillings and ninepence. However, it wasn't long before my drinking took its toll on our marriage. William couldn't handle it anymore, and we separated. With no job or money, I decided to head to Whitechapel to see if I could find work.

I soon discovered that jobs were scarce, and being a woman in those times, I had few options. Desperate for money, I turned to prostitution. It was a risky and dangerous profession, but it was the only way I could make a living. In April 1888, I ended up at the Lambeth workhouse, where the matron found me a position as a domestic servant.

However, my old habits were hard to break, and in just a few weeks, I ran off with clothing worth three pounds and ten shillings. I knew I couldn't go back there, so I returned to Whitechapel.

For a while, I managed to make a decent living as a prostitute. I would spend my days roaming the streets, looking for clients and my nights in the common lodging houses of the area. One night, I had spent all my earnings on gin at the Frying Pan pub in Brick Lane. I left the pub at 12:30 a.m.

, completely drunk, and stumbled into the kitchen of a lodging house on Flower and Dean Street. I was hoping to find a place to sleep for the night, but my plans were thwarted when the deputy lodging house keeper caught me.

He asked if I had my doss money, which was fourpence. When I said, no, he showed me out, warning me not to return until I had my payment. I stumbled out into the dark streets, saying that I would soon find the money. I even proudly pointed to the new black velvet bonnet I had purchased earlier that day on Whitechapel Road and told him, 'See what a jolly bonnet I have now. I'll get my doss money in no time.'

But the truth was, I had little hope of finding enough clients to afford a bed for the night. So I wandered through the streets, drunk and alone. Little did I know that this would be my last night on Earth. The next morning, I was found brutally murdered, my throat slashed and body mutilated.

My murder shocked the entire city, and my name became synonymous with the notorious Jack the Ripper. But I am more than just a victim of a serial killer; I am a woman with a story. A story of a difficult childhood, a troubled marriage, and a life filled with hardship and desperation.

Jack the Ripper – Beyond the Grave

As I look back on my life, I can't help but wonder what could have been if I had made different choices. If I hadn't succumbed to the temptations of alcohol and prostitution, would I have been able to provide for my family and live a decent life?

But it's too late for regrets now. I am at peace, and I rest with the other victims of Jack the Ripper here in heaven. I hope my story serves as a cautionary tale for those who may find themselves in similar circumstances. And I hope that one day, people will remember me for who I was, not just as a footnote in the history of a serial killer.

6

I Meet With an Angel

My name is Charles Lechmere, and I speak to you from beyond the grave. I am here to tell you my story, a story that took place in Victorian London's East End. It was a time and place filled with darkness and despair, but amidst it all, there was still hope and love.

It all started not long after the death of my stepfather. My mother was left alone, and I became the man of the house. I took on the role of provider and protector, and I did everything I could to make sure my mother had everything she needed. That's why, on that particular Sunday afternoon, I found myself walking down the Whitechapel Road, in search of some provisions for my dear mother.

The Whitechapel Road was a busy street, filled with all sorts of shops and businesses. There were cobblers, wheelwrights, greengrocers, and general stores. The streets were also lined with blacksmiths, coopers, and many pub's. But what struck me the most were the many Jewish tailors, their shops filled with vibrant fabrics and intricate designs.

As I walked, I couldn't help but take in the sights and sounds of this bustling street. Omnibuses passed by, pulled by horses, carrying people to different parts of the city. Other horse-drawn vehicles also crowded the road, their sounds and smells filling the air.

I made my way to Williams Tobacconist, a little shop I frequented for my own enjoyment. Mr. Williams, the cheerful bald-headed man who owned the shop, greeted me with a warm smile. I browsed through the various types of pipe tobacco, and admired the different brands of cigarettes and cigars. The shop was filled with the rich scent of tobacco, and I couldn't help but breathe it in deeply.

After purchasing twenty woodbine cigarettes, I left the shop and made my way down the Whitechapel Road once more. As I turned to enter Smith's general store, I accidentally bumped into a young woman. Some of her shopping fell from her basket, and I immediately bent down to pick it up.

The woman had a pretty little face, with large brown eyes that sparkled in the sunlight. She wore a simple Victorian dress, and a dainty little bonnet upon her head, and I couldn't help but admire her. I apologized for my clumsiness, and she smiled at me gratefully. 'Thank you, sir,' she said in a soft voice.

I couldn't help but be drawn to her, and I offered to help her carry her basket. She accepted my offer.

After I had brought my groceries, we started walking together. She told me her name was Elizabeth Bostock, and she lived nearby. As we walked, we chatted about anything and everything, and I found myself completely captivated by her.

When we reached her home, she thanked me and opened the door. I didn't want to leave just yet, so I offered to take her basket into the kitchen for her. She agreed, and I followed her inside. As I placed the basket on the kitchen table, I couldn't help but feel a strong desire to see her again.

Before I left, I mustered up the courage to ask her out on a date. 'I would like to see you again, if you are willing,' I said, my heart pounding in my chest.

She looked at me with her beautiful brown eyes and said, 'I would like that very much, Charlie.'

We arranged to meet the following Sunday, and it was the happiest I had been in a long time. Our date was simple, just a walk in the park and a picnic, but it felt like the most wonderful day of my life. We talked and laughed, and I couldn't help but fall deeper in love with her.

Elizabeth and I continued to see each other, and our love only grew stronger with each passing day. I introduced her to my mother, and she welcomed her with open arms.

Elizabeth and I were happy, and I knew that she was the one I wanted to spend the rest of my life with.

It was a beautiful sunny day in the city and I found myself walking towards Elizabeth's door, as I did every week for our scheduled dates. We had been seeing each other for a few weeks now and I couldn't help but feel like I was falling for her more and more with each passing day.

As soon as she opened the door, a smile spread across her face and I knew that I was in for another wonderful day. We walked down the streets towards the busier parts of the city, chatting and laughing along the way. Elizabeth always had a way of making me feel at ease, like I could be myself without any judgment.

I took her to a nearby Italian café for some tea and cakes, one of our favorite places to go. As soon as we walked in, the delicious smell of freshly brewed coffee hit me and I couldn't help but take a deep breath, savoring the aroma. We sat down at a cozy table and the waitress came over to take our order. The display of colorful cakes and pastries in the glass counter in front of us was simply irresistible. We ended up ordering a variety of cakes to share, from rich chocolate cakes to delicate fruit tarts.

As we indulged in our sweet treats, Elizabeth and I chatted about everything and anything. She told me about her family and her dreams for the future, while I shared stories from my childhood and my job at the local Pickford's Depot. We laughed and joked, lost in each other's company.

Afterwards, we decided to take a walk in the nearby park. The sun was shining and the park was in full bloom with beautiful flowers of every color.

Elizabeth and I strolled hand in hand, admiring the scenery and enjoying the peaceful atmosphere. We even stopped to watch the graceful swans swimming in the lake.

Eventually, we made our way to the city zoo. Elizabeth had never been to a zoo before, so I was excited to show her all the different animals. We saw everything from fierce tigers to adorable penguins. Elizabeth's eyes lit up with wonder and joy as she saw each new exhibit.

As we sat on a wooden bench under the shade of a tree, Elizabeth turned to me and thanked me for taking her to so many wonderful places. Then she said something that surprised me, 'Do you know Charlie, I have never been into a public house in my life.' Her admission made me instantly decide that she needed to have that experience.

'I'll take you to one next week, if you'd like,' I told her with a mischievous grin. She hesitated at first, but eventually agreed to go.

The following Sunday afternoon, I arrived at Elizabeth's door at noon just as I had promised. We set off towards the Alma, a pub that I knew had a reputation for very little trouble. As we entered the pub, the smell of beer and the lively atmosphere hit us. I could see that Elizabeth was a little nervous but I reassured her that it would be fine.

We sat at a table in the corner and ordered our drinks. As we sipped our drinks, I noticed my uncle Sid with some of the slaughter men that he worked with, talking to four women at the bar. They were definitely prostitutes, dressed in revealing clothing and heavy makeup. My uncle didn't see me, but I couldn't help but feel a sense of discomfort knowing that he was associating with such women.

Suddenly, each of the prostitutes got up and took their clients out of the pub, my uncle included. I could see them laughing and joking as they left and I felt a sense of unease wash over me. I turned to Elizabeth and asked her if she would excuse me for a moment. I walked over to the bar and asked the barman the names of the prostitutes.

He pointed to each of them as he spoke, 'From left to right, that's Annie Chapman, Elizabeth Stride, Catherine Eddowes, and the pretty one is Mary Jane Kelly.' I couldn't believe my luck. Little did they know, from that day on each one would be added to my list of victims. and I shall tell you the reason why very soon.

7

Annie Chapman – from Beyond the Grave

My name is Annie Chapman, and I speak to you from beyond the grave. I was born in Paddington, London on the 25th September 1840, to George Smith and Ruth Chapman. My father was a soldier of the 2nd Regiment of Life Guards. I was the first of five children, but my family was not traditional. My parents were not married at the time of my birth, but they did eventually marry two years later.

We lived a relatively comfortable life in Paddington, as my father's position in the army allowed us to live in a nice house. However, when my father left the army, things changed for us. He was able to secure a position as a valet, but it meant that we had to leave our home in Paddington and move to Berkshire.

It was here that I first tasted alcohol, and unfortunately, I developed a weakness for spirit, especially Rum. My siblings would often find me drunk and lecture me about the dangers of alcohol.

They even made me sign a pledge to stop drinking, which I did, but the demon drinks' call was too great, and I started drinking once more.

In 1861, my family moved to Clewer, and I made the decision to move to London. I was not content with living in the countryside and wanted to experience the excitement of city life. I was able to secure a position as a domestic servant, and it was then that I met John James Chapman.

John was related to my mother, and we soon fell in love. We were married on 1st May 1869, at All Saints Church in

Knightsbridge. We moved into a small house at 29 Montpellier Place and started our family. We had three children, Emily, Annie, and John Jr. Unfortunately, John Jr. was born a cripple and required constant care and attention.

As I was busy with taking care of my children and household duties, my drinking began to slow down. By 1880, I was nearly dry, but the stress and constant struggle of raising a disabled child started to take its toll on me. I found myself turning to alcohol once again for comfort.

In 1882, we experienced a great tragedy when our daughter Emily passed away from meningitis. My husband and I were devastated, and we turned to drinking as a means of numbing our pain. We started drinking more heavily, and it began to affect our relationship.

I was arrested many times for drunken and disorderly behavior, but I never appeared before a magistrate. My husband and I just couldn't seem to break the cycle of alcohol abuse. In 1884, we decided to separate, and my children went to live with my husband.

Without my family or a stable source of income, I moved to the East End of London and started living in common lodging houses in Whitechapel and Spitalfields. It was a far cry from the comfortable life I had once known. With no job and a constant need for alcohol, I turned to prostitution to make ends meet. I would often drink my earnings and end up sleeping rough on the streets.

One evening in the pub, I got into a fight with another prostitute named Eliza Cooper. We were both heavily intoxicated and ended up causing a commotion. The fight spilled out onto the street, and a group of men had to break it up, and I stumbled away with a black eye.

Despite my struggles, I still had hope for a better life. I held onto my memories of my children and the love I had for them. But as the years went by and my situation became increasingly dire, I lost the will to live. I turned to alcohol as a means of escape and became a permanent resident of the local doss house.

Eventually, my health began to fail, and I knew my time was coming to an end. On the early morning of September 8th, 1888, my body was discovered in a doorway on Hanbury Street in Whitechapel. I was brutally murdered by the infamous serial killer known as Jack the Ripper.

Even in death, my story is one of tragedy and struggle. But my hope is that by sharing my story, I can serve as a cautionary tale of the dangers of alcohol and the destructive path it can lead you down. Hold onto your loved ones and never let go, for in the end, they are all that truly matters. As for me, I will forever be remembered as Annie Chapman, a victim of Jack the Ripper. But I was more than just a victim. I was a mother, a wife, and a woman who lived and loved despite the hardships I faced. May my story serve as a testament to the strength and resilience of the human spirit.

8
Charles Allen Lechmere – from Beyond the Grave

My name is Charles Allen Lechmere, and I speak to you from beyond the grave. You may know of me as one of history's most notorious serial killers, Jack the Ripper. But that is not the story that I wish to tell. No, I want to tell you about my life before the darkness consumed me, and I became known as Jack the Ripper.

As I have told in my story so far, I met and fell in love with a beautiful, young woman called Elizabeth. And we courted for a year, getting to know each other and discovering our love for one another. Finally, I mustered the courage to propose, and she accepted. We were married on the 3rd of July 1870 at Christ Church in the parish of St George in the East union. Our wedding was a small affair, with only close friends and family in attendance.

But it was a day that I will never forget. My heart swelled with love for my new bride, and I knew that my life would be changed forever.

We didn't have much money, so we lived with my mother for a few years after getting married. It was a humble life, but we were happy. We then moved to a rented property at 22 Doveton Street in the East End. It was a modest home, but it was ours. And it was there that we started our family.

Between 1872 and 1891, Elizabeth and I had eleven children. Their names were Charles, Elizabeth, Emily, Jane, Thomas. George, William, James, Louisa, Charles Allen (named after myself), Albert, and Harriet Emma. Our first child, Charles, was named after me, but sadly we lost him to consumption when he was only three years old. It was a devastating blow to our family, but we found solace in our other children.

Elizabeth Emily was named after my beloved sister, who had passed away. She was a kind and gentle soul, and I wanted to honor her memory in any way I could. Jane was the spitting image of her mother, with her jet black hair and dark brown eyes.

Thomas was named after my stepfather, who had been a father figure to me when I was young.

My boys, George, William, James, and Albert, were all strong and healthy. They were full of energy and mischief, but they brought so much joy to our lives. Louisa, our youngest daughter, was named after my mother. She was a lively and spirited girl, with a mischievous glint in her eye.

But our family was not without tragedy. In 1890, our daughter Harriet Emma passed away. It was a difficult time for all of us, especially Elizabeth. She was devastated by the loss of her sweet little girl. But in 1891, Elizabeth fell pregnant again, and we knew that this would be our last chance to have another child. And so, when our daughter was born, we named her Harriet Emma in memory of the daughter we had lost the year before.

As our children grew up, Elizabeth and I watched with pride. Charles, our eldest, followed in my footsteps and became a carter. He was a hardworking and dedicated young man, just like his father. Elizabeth Emily had a passion for art, and we encouraged her to pursue her dreams.

Jane had a talent for singing, and she would often perform for us in the evenings. Thomas went on to become a policeman, and my stepfather couldn't have been prouder. Our boys, George, William, James, and Albert, all found their own paths in life. They were all good and kind-hearted men.

As for Louisa, she had a wild and adventurous spirit. She was always seeking new thrills and pushing the boundaries. But she was also fiercely protective of her younger siblings and would do anything for them.

And so, our family continued to grow and flourish. We had our ups and downs, our joys and sorrows, but through it all, we had each other. Elizabeth and I loved each other more with each passing day, and our family was the center of our world.

And as I lay here in my grave, I am grateful for the life I lived before the darkness consumed me and I became known as Jack the Ripper.

9

Elizabeth Stride
– from Beyond the Grave

My name is Elizabeth Stride, and I speak to you from beyond the grave. My story begins in the small rural village of Stora Tumlehed in Sweden. I was born on November 27th, 1843 to Gustaf Ericsson, a farmer, and my mother Beata. I was the second eldest of four children, and we were brought up in the Lutheran faith.

Growing up, my siblings and I were expected to help out on the farm, and I learned how to do many chores from a young age. At the age of fifteen, I was confirmed at the church of Torslanda, and the following year I decided to leave my village in search of employment in the city of Gothenburg.

I quickly found a job as a domestic worker for a couple named Olofsson. They were kind and treated me well, but the wages were not enough to support my habits. You see, I had a problem with drinking, and it became worse as I grew older. I found myself roaming the streets in the evenings and on my days off, offering my services as a prostitute in order to make more money.

I was arrested a number of times for prostitution, but it didn't stop me from continuing. In 1864, my mother passed away, leaving me with an inheritance of 65 krona. However, due to legal complications, I didn't receive the money until late 1865. With that money, I made a decision that would change the course of my life - I moved to London.

I arrived in London with no knowledge of the English language, but I was determined to make a new life for myself. I quickly learned the language and became quite fluent, although I could never get rid of the slight Swedish twang in my voice. In 1869, I met John Thomas Stride, a ship's carpenter, and we quickly fell in love. We got married a month later on the 7th of March in St Giles in the Field church.

Together, we opened a small coffee shop on Poplar high street. For a while, everything seemed perfect - I had a loving husband, a successful business, and a new home in a big city. But as time went on, our marriage began to decline. John was 22 years older than me and we had very different personalities. By 1874, our marriage had completely fallen apart, and John closed the business in 1875.

With no stable income and no husband to support me, I found myself back on the streets of Whitechapel, working as a prostitute once again. I moved from one lodging house to another, trying to make enough money to buy a little food, and the fourpence I needed so I could have a bed for the night in one of the local doss houses. But my drinking habits often took preference, and I found myself sleeping on the streets.

Life on the streets of Whitechapel was rough - violence, crime, and poverty were a daily occurrence. Prostitution was a common way for women to earn money, but it was also incredibly dangerous. Many of my friends and fellow prostitutes were victims of violence and abuse. Despite the dangers, I couldn't give up my habits and continued working as a prostitute for many years.

In 1888, a series of brutal murders shook the streets of Whitechapel. It became known as the 'Whitechapel murders' or the 'Jack the Ripper killings'. The victims were all female prostitutes, and I knew all of them personally. I was terrified that I would be next, but I couldn't stop my lifestyle.

On the night of September 30th, 1888, I went out as usual, hoping to make some money. Little did I know that it would be my last night alive. I was found dead in Dutfield's Yard the next morning, my throat had been slashed.

Many theories surrounded my death, and the identity of Jack the Ripper remains a mystery to this day. But I know the truth - I was just a woman trying to survive in a harsh and unforgiving world. I speak from beyond the grave to tell my story, to share the struggles of women like myself who were forced into prostitution due to poverty and addiction.

My name is Elizabeth Stride, and I may have been known as 'Long Liz' in London, but to those who loved me, I was just a woman trying to make the best of a difficult life. May my story be a reminder that every person has a story, and no one should be judged for the choices they make to survive.

10
Charles Allen Lechmere – from Beyond the Grave

My name is Charles Allen Lechmere, and I speak to you from beyond the grave. As I have told, Elizabeth and I had moved into our own home at 22 Doveton Street in London, and our family started to flourish. My Elizabeth was a good wife and mother, and she kept a tidy house. She was also a fantastic cook, whipping up the most delicious meals for me and our children. I looked forward to coming home in the evenings, greeted by the warmth of our fire and the sound of my family's laughter.

After dinner, once the children had kissed me goodnight and gone to bed, Elizabeth and I would sit by the fire and I would read the newspaper to her. You see, Elizabeth could neither read nor write, as was the case with so many people in the East End. We spent our evenings chatting and laughing, enjoying each other's company. It was during these moments of peace and calm that the voices in my head started to return. They came back louder and more frequent than ever before, a constant nagging in the back of my mind. I knew that the time for vengeance was drawing near.

The voices spoke to me day and night, urging me to take revenge on those who had wronged me. The filthy whores of the East End, they would pay for their sins. I could feel my anger growing, a seething hatred that consumed me. Oh, how I longed to make them suffer. Their time was drawing near.

I began to make my plans. I knew I had to take my vengeance upon my way to work, and I knew exactly how to do it. You see, my job as a carter required me to leave early in the morning and return late in the evening. This provided the perfect cover for my actions. I would leave at three in the morning, and on my forty-five minute walk through the dark streets of Whitechapel, I would have more than enough time to carry out my plans.

I had the perfect disguise. My clothes were always stained with blood, the result of working as a carter and handling animal carcasses. And my long apron, worn to protect my clothing, always had a dark stain of blood upon it, no matter how many times Elizabeth washed it. It was the perfect place to conceal a weapon.

On my next day off, I set out to Whitechapel Road and bought a long knife at the ironmongers. It was a beautiful weapon, with a blade around eight inches long and a pure leather sheath. I was in awe of its sharpness and strength. I knew this was the perfect weapon for my revenge. With my new purchase safely hidden in the coal shed, I started making my plans.

I scouted the area, looking for my targets. I knew their routines, where they worked, where they lived. I made detailed notes, tracking their movements and habits. I was meticulous in my planning, leaving nothing to chance. I wanted to make sure that my revenge would be swift and merciless.

As the days went by, my thirst for revenge grew stronger. I could feel the darkness within me reaching a boiling point, aching to be unleashed. I felt alive, empowered by the thought of making those women pay for the pain they had caused me. It was a cold, foggy morning in Victorian London and I had just awoken from my slumber. I quietly slipped out of bed, careful not to wake my wife, Elizabeth, who was a heavy sleeper. She would never know that I started leaving the house at an ungodly hour for the past few months.

I had taken to leaving at three in the morning, opening the front door very quietly so as not to disturb my dear wife. I would slip out into the quiet streets, making my way to certain spots along my route to work. As I walked, I couldn't help but remember the late nights I spent as a young boy, walking with my stepfather

Thomas Cross, a police constable whose patrols were in the Whitechapel area.

In those days, I had been fascinated by my stepfather's job and would often accompany him on his nightly rounds. I remember the dark streets, the eerie silence, and the occasional sound of footsteps in the distance. It was during those walks that I had first noticed the other policemen patrolling the area. I had made it my mission to observe and learn their routines, their timings, and their routes.

And now, after all these years, I found myself walking the same streets, but this time with a purpose. I wanted to see if the times of the other policemen had changed. So, for the past few months, I had been stopping for about half an hour or so, hiding in the shadows and watching as the bobbies walked their beat.

I would take notes, jotting down the times that each Bobby passed a certain point of the street. And over the many nights that I stood in the shadows, I found that I could set my watch by the bobbies' return to the same spot, give or take a minute or two. It was a precise routine, and I was amazed at how accurate I had become at predicting their movements.

As the months went by, I continued to watch and record the times of each bobbies' return. I grew to memorize their schedules, noting the exact times they passed through each street. I would even repeat the timings to myself over and over again, until I had them all committed to memory.

It was a peculiar hobby, and many would find it strange that I spent my early mornings, lurking in the shadows and watching policemen walk their beat. But to me, it was a game, a challenge. And as I watched night after night, I began to notice small changes in their patterns. A few minutes here, a different route there.

I couldn't help but wonder what had caused these slight changes. Was it due to new orders from the police station? Or were they trying to avoid a certain area for some reason? My curiosity only grew stronger as I continued to observe and record the bobbies' movements.

From that day on, I continued my early morning routine with a newfound purpose. I had found a way to avoid the crowded streets and reach my destination in record time. And as I walked past the familiar spots where I used to hide, watching the policemen on their beats, I couldn't help but smile to myself.

I had discovered a way to outsmart the bobbies of Victorian London, and it was all thanks to my early morning routine. To those around me, I was just an ordinary man, but little did they know, I was a master of the streets, hiding in the shadows and watching everything that went on in the dark corners of the city.

11

Catherine Eddowes – from Beyond the Grave

My name is Catherine Eddowes, and I speak to you from beyond the grave. My story begins in the small village of Graisley Green in Wolverhampton where I was born on 14th April 1842. My parents, George and Catherine Eddowes, were hard-working individuals. My father was a tinplate worker while my mother worked as a cook at the Peacock Hotel. I was one of twelve children in the Eddowes family, born into a modest life but surrounded by love and laughter.

In 1843, my family packed up and moved to London in search of better work opportunities. My father secured a job at a firm called Perkins and Sharpus in Bell Court. We settled in a small house at 4 Baden Place in Bermondsey, with its cramped rooms and narrow alleyways. Our family later moved to a larger house at 35 West Street, which we were all excited about. But our joy was short-lived when my mother passed away in 1855, at the young age of 42, from consumption.

Two years later, my father also fell ill and passed away. With both parents gone, my siblings and I were admitted to the Bermondsey workhouse as orphans. It was a difficult time for us as we were separated and forced to do laborious tasks to earn our keep. However, a glimmer of hope came when we were accepted into a local industrial school, where we were taught a trade in hope of securing a better future.

I was determined to make something of myself, and after leaving the school, I landed a job as a tinplate stamper at the Old Hall Works. I was proud to have a steady job and was content with my simple life.

However, my temptation to steal got the better of me, and I was caught and subsequently fired. I was devastated at losing my job, but I had no one but myself to blame.

I felt like a failure and had nowhere to turn. That was when my uncle, who lived in Birmingham, offered me a place to stay. He was a shoemaker and provided me with a job as a tray polisher on Legge Street. I was grateful for his help, and I vowed to work hard and make a better life for myself.

Things took a turn for the better when I met Thomas Conway, a soldier in the 18th Royal Irish Regiment. We fell in love, and soon after, we got married. We were blessed with two beautiful children, Catherine Ann and Thomas Lawrence. However, our happiness was short-lived as Thomas was often away on duty, leaving me to care for the children and household alone.

In 1868, Thomas was relocated to London, and naturally, we followed. However, the big city proved to be a temptation that I could not resist. I began to frequent the local pubs, and soon, the demon drink took hold of me. I was often seen with black eyes and bruises on my face from quarrels with Thomas. Our relationship became tumultuous, and the violence escalated as my drinking habits worsened.

In 1880, I could no longer take the abuse, and I made the difficult decision to leave Thomas. I moved to the East End of London, the heart of the city's poverty and desperation. With limited job opportunities, I turned to prostitution to support myself. I also took on casual work when I could find it, but it was not enough to sustain me.

I began to spend my nights in the local doss houses, the only place I could afford with my limited income. But if I drank away my earnings, I would spend the night in the front room of a lodging house on 26 Dorset Street, known as 'the Shed'. It was a squalid and miserable existence, but it was all I had.

As the years went by, my drinking habits only got worse, and my body began to suffer the consequences. My once beautiful appearance was now marred by the effects of alcohol, and my health deteriorated rapidly. My life was spiraling out of control, and I seemed to have no way out. I was lost and alone in the vast city of London, with no family or friends to turn to.

But little did I know that my life was about to take a tragic and gruesome turn. On the night of 30th September 1888, my body was discovered in a dark corner of Mitre Square, brutally murdered by a killer who would later be known as 'Jack the Ripper.' My final hours were spent in fear and terror, and as I took my last breath, I wondered what could have been if I had made different choices in my life.

Now, as I speak to you from beyond the grave, I can reflect on my life and the circumstances that led me to my tragic end. I regret the mistakes I made and the pain I caused to those around me. I can only hope that my story serves as a cautionary tale for those who may be tempted to make the same choices I did.

And as for Jack the Ripper, he may have taken my life, but he will never silence my voice. I will forever be remembered as Catherine Eddowes, a daughter, a mother, a wife, a victim, and a voice from beyond the grave.

12

I Meet With a Devil

My name is Charles Allen Lechmere, and I speak to you from beyond the grave. I was a simple cart driver for Pickford's Depot in the bustling city of London. It was a hard job, but it paid well and I enjoyed working with the horses. It was a peaceful day as I made my way through the streets of Islington, heading back to the depot after making my deliveries.

The sun was shining and the streets were bustling with people going about their daily routines. I had my two magnificent shire horses, Goliath and his sister Sheba, with me that day. They were strong and reliable, and I trusted them to get me safely to my destination.

I was passing by Elizabeth Terrace when I noticed a group of children playing on the pavement. They were laughing and shouting, completely oblivious to the world around them. I slowed my cart down, not wanting to startle them, and continued down Liverpool Street.

As I turned the corner, I spotted a woman at the corner of the street. It was clear to me that she was a prostitute, her clothes were revealing and her demeanor was loud and unapologetic. It was also clear that she was very drunk, leaning against the wall for support.

As I watched the children play, the woman began to shout at them. 'Piss off ya little bleeders, bugger off, you're putting off me customers!' she slurred, trying to chase them away. The children paid her no mind and continued to play, causing an even bigger ruckus.

Suddenly, one of the boys darted out from the woman's reach and ran out into the road. I tried to stop the horses, but it was too late. The wheel of my cart went over the little boy, and I could hear his bones crack under the weight.

I quickly jumped down from the cart and rushed over to the boy. He was in a bad way, with blood pooling onto the cobbled street. The prostitute stumbled over and looked at the dying boy with disgust. 'Serves the little bugger right, spoiling my chances of picking up a punter,' she spat before staggering off down the street.

I was shaken and horrified by her callousness. I stayed by the boy's side until the police arrived, telling them what had happened and describing the woman who had caused the accident. They immediately recognized her as Polly Nichols.

The boy was taken to the hospital, but unfortunately, he did not survive. My heart ached for him and his family. They would never know that their child's death was caused by a careless and selfish woman.

The police soon found Polly Nichols, and brought her in for questioning. I was brought in as a witness and recounted what had happened. The woman showed no remorse for her actions and even laughed at the boy's death, saying that it was his own fault for running into the road.

I was then told that I had to appear at the coroner's court on Wednesday next. The day finally arrived and I was brought in to testify about the incident. I retold my side of the story, including Polly's involvement, but the court did not seem to think she was to blame. She was not called as a witness and was subsequently released.

Next up was a man named George Porter. He claimed to have been outside his brother's shop, 3 Elizabeth Terrace, on the day of the accident. He said that he saw the child run into the road and that I had called out to them, but it was too late. The child was already under my cart's wheels.

Another witness, Henrietta Owen, was then questioned. She stated that my cart was going at a slow pace and that, in her opinion, I was not at fault. Then came William Warner, who said that he had heard me shouting, but the cart was already upon the child.

The jury listened intently and then expressed their opinion that I was not to blame. They returned a verdict of accidental death and I was told that I could go. The whole hearing had only lasted about half an hour. I could not believe it had ended so quickly. I felt a mixture of relief and disbelief that I had been cleared of any wrongdoing.

Upon reaching the street, I decided to go to a nearby pub for a stiff drink. As I sat there, nursing my drink and still reeling from the events of the day, something inside me snapped. Those bastards in the court didn't care about little Walter Williams who had died beneath my wheels. They had simply brushed it off as an accident and moved on. My rage started to simmer once more, and I made a decision right then and there.

Polly Nichols and all those who had wronged me would pay. I had an ever-growing list of victims and I made it my mission to seek revenge on every single one of them. They would pay with their lives, just like Walter Williams had paid with his.

And so began my descent into darkness. I became a vigilante, targeting those who had wronged me and others in the city. I took justice into my own hands and left a trail of bodies in my wake. The city was in chaos and people lived in fear of JACK THE RIPPER.

13

Mary Jane Kelly
– from Beyond the Grave

My name is Mary Jane Kelly, and I speak to you from beyond the grave. My life on earth began in 1863, in the small town of Limerick, Ireland. I was the youngest child of John and Martha Kelly, and I had seven brothers and one sister. My family was not wealthy, but my father had a respectable job in an ironworks, and we were considered well-off in our small community.

Growing up, my parents were very strict and brought us up in the Catholic faith. We were expected to attend church every Sunday, unless we were feeling ill. It didn't take long for me to figure out that faking illness was the best way to avoid attending church. While my parents were at church, I would sneak down to the living room and help myself to the alcohol cabinet. At first, it was just a sip or two, but as time went on, I found myself becoming addicted to alcohol.

As I grew into my teenage years, my sneaking became more frequent and my addiction grew stronger. I would tell my parents that I was going to town, only to go straight to the off-licence and buy myself a bottle of gin. I would then smuggle the bottle back into our home. This went on for some time, and more than once my father caught me in a drunken state and unleashed his anger onto me. I was also known to cause trouble while under the influence and had to be collected from town on several occasions.

My father had finally had enough and decided to disown me when I was only 16 years old. He told me he never wanted to see me again, and I was forced to leave our family home. I found work in a factory in a small mining town, where I met a miner named John Davis. We fell in love and got married, but only two years later, John was killed in a mining accident.

With no means of support, I moved to Cardiff, but I struggled to find work. In desperation, I turned to prostitution to make ends meet.

In 1884, I moved to the bustling city of London, hoping to find better job opportunities. I first found work in a Tobacconist, but I was eventually dismissed for helping myself to stock. I then found a job as a domestic servant in Crispin Street, but I was once again fired for helping myself to drink.

With no other options, I decided to join the ranks of high-class prostitutes in London's West End.

I became one of the most popular girls at the brothel and earned a fair wage, which I spent on expensive clothes and accessories. To appeal to my wealthy clients, I adopted the name 'Marie Jeanette.' My life was finally looking up, and I had everything I had ever wanted - money, freedom, and the ability to indulge in my vices without any consequences.

With the money I earned, I was able to rent a comfortable room near the London Docks. Mrs. Buki, my landlady, was a kind woman who took me in as if I was her own. I was happy with my life at that time, enjoying the finer things in life that I had always dreamed of. But as time went by, my drinking habits started to become worse.

I then moved to Breezer's Hill and rented another room from Mrs. Carthy, a fellow Irish woman. I lived there for a year before I met Edward Morganstone. He was a charming man, and I couldn't resist his charm. We fell in love and moved in together in a room near the commercial gas works in Stepney. But unfortunately, we were both heavy drinkers, and within a few months, our relationship ended in a fiery mess.

Heartbroken and alone, I met Joseph Flemming, a mason's plasterer, and moved in with him. Again, we were both heavy drinkers, and our relationship didn't last long. In the span of just a few weeks, we both realized that we were not meant for each other.

By this time, it was 1886, and I had hit rock bottom. I was living in Cooley's lodging house in Thrawl Street, Spitalfields, and walking the streets as a prostitute to make ends meet. It was a dangerous and tough life, but I didn't have any other options.

On April 8th, 1887, I met Joseph Barnett on Commercial Street. He was a fish porter at Billingsgate market, and he took me for a drink. I liked him immediately, and we agreed to live together in George Street. I was honest with him about my profession, but he didn't seem to mind as long as I brought in money for us to survive.

We were both heavy drinkers, and as our relationship progressed, our drinking habits became even worse. We moved from one rented room to another, struggling to pay our rent and keep ourselves fed. Eventually, we found a single room in Little Paternoster Row, but our constant arguments and Joseph's job loss due to theft led to our eviction.

In March of 1888, we moved to 13 Miller's Court, off Dorset Street, in Spitalfields. It was a small and sparsely furnished room, but it was all we could afford. The weekly rent was four shillings and sixpence, and we both knew it was a stretch for us to afford. But we didn't have much of a choice.

When I was alone in the room, I would often sing the songs of my homeland, reminiscing about the life I once had before coming to London. The room had a bed, three tables, and a single chair, but it was all I needed to feel at home.

But after a week or two, the arguments between Joseph and me started again. He lost his job, and we were both struggling to make ends meet. As time went by, our relationship became strained, and in July 1888, Joseph finally left me. I was heartbroken and felt completely alone. I wished I had enough money to return to Ireland, but my drinking habits had taken their toll on my finances.

I was now living in the infamous Whitechapel district, where murder and crime were a common occurrence. But it was all I had known for the past few years. I had no family or friends to turn to, and my only means of survival was by selling my body.

Living a life of poverty and hardship in 1880s London had taken a toll on me. My once youthful and striking appearance was slowly fading away, and my drinking habits had only added to my troubles. But little did I know that the end of my life was approaching, and my name would go down in history as one of the victims of the infamous Jack the Ripper.

14

Murder

– But Not By My Hands

My name is Charles Allen Lechmere, and I speak to you from beyond the grave. I will tell you now about the news of 1887. I had finished at my place of work on the 23rd December. And I was enjoying the Christmas holiday with my wife and children. My mother was then remarried to a nice man by the name of Joseph Forsdike, a shoemaker. Both came and spent Christmas with us, and were staying with us until the 27th December. It was on this day I had returned to my work as a carman, and my mother and her husband stayed until the evening of that day.

Upon my way home, I stopped and bought a newspaper, and tucking it under my arm, I walked the many roads of the East End. It was a cold night in London, and the streets were filled with people rushing to get to their destinations before the snow started to fall. As I finally arrived at my doorstep, I found my dinner waiting for me. After dinner, I retired to the living room and joined Elizabeth my wife, and my mother and stepfather, who were all sitting around the fire.

After a little talking, Joseph, my stepfather, said, 'I see you have bought a copy of the evening news, have you taken a look at it yet?' I told him no, as I was waiting for the right moment to read it. My wife then suggested that I read the newspaper to them, as only my mother and I could read and write. I agreed, and started to read through the newspaper, telling them about the different stories within its pages. Assault in Kensington. Mugging in the west end. Murderer hanged at Newgate prison. Four women charged with prostitution. Bank robbed at gunpoint. But it wasn't until I reached the center pages that I suddenly stopped reading, wondering why I had suddenly become silent. My wife asked me what was wrong, and after a few seconds, I started to read.

'Brutal murder in Commercial Road alley,' I read aloud. 'On Boxing Day night, the body of a woman was found lying in an alleyway off Commercial Road. Police investigating the murder think it to be the work of pimps who the deceased owed money. The police have named the deceased as Fairy Fay, a well known prostitute of the East End.

I couldn't believe it. Someone else had killed the whore before me. My heart sank, and I couldn't help but feel a sense of disappointment. I had always wanted to be the one to end her miserable existence, to rid the world of her filth and disease. But here she was, dead at the hands of someone else. I couldn't help but think, 'Why couldn't it be me?'

My mother and stepfather were watching me closely, probably wondering why I had suddenly become quiet again. But they couldn't possibly understand the complex emotions that were going through my mind at that moment.

I couldn't help but feel a sense of jealousy and anger towards her killer. I wanted to be the one to bring an end to her reign on the streets of London.

As the evening went on, my thoughts were consumed by Fairy Fay. My wife, mother, and stepfather were talking about the upcoming New Year's celebrations, but I couldn't bring myself to join in the conversation. I excused myself and went to bed, only to be haunted by thoughts of Fairy Fay, and my failure to claim her life.

It was April 1888 when I heard the news from my uncle Sid. He was always eager to chat with me on my way home from work, and this time he had a story that would change the course of my life. As I walked along the bustling streets of East End London, he told me about a prostitute named Emma Smith who had been brutally murdered on the 4th of April.

Uncle Sid's recount of the events was both shocking and intriguing. Emma had been found with severe injuries, her attacker had knocked her over the head and thrust something hard up between her legs, causing massive internal bleeding. Despite managing to make it home, she had not survived the loss of blood and had passed away a few hours later.

As I listened to my uncle's description of the horrific scene, my mind began to spin. I too, like many others in this part of London, had a deep- rooted hatred towards prostitutes. They were a nuisance, always lingering on the streets and tempting men away from their families. I had even devised a plan to rid East End of this filth, but it seemed someone else had beaten me to it.

I bid my uncle farewell and made my way along Bucks Row, my mind filled with anger at the thought that someone else had taken the life of a prostitute that I had been planning to kill. It should have been me, I thought to myself. But the realization that someone else had the same idea fueled a fire within me. I vowed to make all the whores on my list suffer, not just with death but with merciless torture.

The voices in my head were now screaming at me, urging me to take revenge. And what revenge I will take, I thought to myself. I knew that my killing spree in the East End would go down in history as the most notorious one the world had ever known. Every man, woman, and child would talk about me and my actions for hundreds, if not thousands of years to come. I would be remembered as a legend, a man who stood up against the filth that threatened society.

With my mind set on revenge, I continued to walk home, my footsteps echoing through the empty streets of the East End. Once inside my humble abode, I began to make plans for my notorious killing spree. I wanted to make sure that every detail was perfectly executed, from choosing the right victims to the methods of torture I would use. These prostitutes had it coming, and they would soon realize the true consequences of their actions.

The days turned into weeks, and finally, it was time to put my plan into action. I had meticulously selected my first victim, Martha Tabram.

***

I always knew my uncle Sid was not a respectable man. He had always been a bit rough around the edges, with a hard attitude and a tendency to speak his mind. But I never expected to receive the news I did on this particular Sunday in July of 1888.

It was a hot day, the sun beating down on the crowded streets of Whitechapel. I had just finished filling the coal bucket, when there was a knock on the door. It was one of the men who worked with my uncle at the abattoir. He looked grim as he told me that my uncle Sid was very ill and that the doctor had given him only a short time to live.

Shocked, I thanked the man and went inside, telling my wife that I needed to go see my uncle.

Making my way through the dirty streets, I couldn't help but think about my uncle. He was known as a hard but honest man, never one to shy away from a hard day's work. But he was also known for his love of women. I never judged him for it, knowing that he was a single man and could do as he pleased.

I arrived at my uncle's lodgings and was let in by Mrs. Simpson, the landlady. She led me up to my uncle's room and left me alone with him. As soon as I walked in, I could tell that he was not doing well. He had lost a lot of weight since the last time I had seen him, and there were nasty red sores covering his body. The room was stifling hot, and I could see the sweat trickling down his face.

'Hello, Charlie boy,' he said weakly as he welcomed me in. I sat down on the side of his bed, trying not to show my shock at his appearance.

'What did the doctor say?' I asked, trying to keep my voice steady.

My uncle looked into my eyes and sighed. 'I've got a dose of the clap, Charlie. It's me own fault.'

My mind reeled at the news. Syphilis was a disease I knew of, but I never expected my own uncle to have it.

He let out a deep breath and began to explain. 'Well, Charlie boy, as you know, I have never married.

And I have always been a one for the ladies. But you see, ever since I was young, I couldn't keep a girl. As soon as I tried it on, the decent girls I met would run a mile.'

I nodded, understanding what he meant. Our neighborhood was not the best, and decent women were hard to come by.

'So I thought to myself, who needs a decent girl when I could get what I wanted for just a few pennies? There would be no arguments or paying out on fancy meals and such. So I started using four of the local girls, if you know what I mean.'

My uncle's words didn't shock me. He had been paying for the services of prostitutes for years.

'I've been lucky until now,' my uncle continued. 'But I suppose my luck has run out.'

I couldn't help but feel disgusted and ashamed of my uncle's actions. But then a thought struck me. If he had been using prostitutes for years, how many other men in our neighborhood had been doing the same? And how many of those whores had spread this terrible disease.

'Uncle Sid, can you tell me the names of these women?' I asked, my mind already forming a plan to bring justice upon those foul bitches.

My uncle looked at me with a small smile. 'You know them, Charlie. You must have seen me with them at some time or another. I never made a secret of it. Long Liz Stride, little Annie Chapman, Catherine Eddowes, and the tall, pretty Irish lass, Mary Kelly.'

I felt a chill run down my spine as he spoke those names. I remembered that time when I had taken my then-girlfriend to the Alma public house, and I had seen my uncle from a corner of the room, laughing and joking with the prostitutes before leaving with them.

Leaving my uncle's bedside, I made my way back home. My list of victims now numbered six, and very soon I would take their lives. My uncle passed away two weeks later, and the voices within my head started screaming even louder, to take vengeance upon those bitches that had taken him from me.

15
The Murder of Martha Tabram

My name is Charles Allen Lechmere, and I speak to you from beyond the grave. 3 a.m. on the 6th of August, 1888. I had risen early, closed my door quietly behind me, and started my journey through the dark, dirty streets of Whitechapel. It was a warm, humid night and the streets were deserted. I could feel my heart beating within my chest as I made my way along the dimly lit streets of the East End.

The gas street lamps provided only a faint glow, spaced far apart in this part of the city. This suited my purpose for tonight, as I was out to make my first kill. The streets were eerily quiet, save for the occasional sound of drunken laughter or the shuffling of feet from the many pubs that were still doing a roaring trade, even at this ungodly hour.

I made my way to a place in the shadows opposite the Angel and Crown pub. From the darkness, I watched the pub, biding my time. A police officer passed the pub, carrying on down the street before disappearing into the night. I checked my pocket watch and knew he would not return for another twenty-five minutes to half an hour. I smirked to myself, knowing I had picked the perfect time to strike.

I continued to keep a watchful eye from the shadows of the alleyway. Within five minutes, I saw her - Martha Tabram. She staggered out of the pub, her movements sluggish from the alcohol she had consumed. I looked around, making sure no one was watching before I approached her.

'Come on deary,' she slurred, 'let Martha take care of you. It will only cost you a few pennies.'

I played along, pretending to be a willing customer. She led me to a dark, secluded area known as George Yard Buildings and up a flight of stairs to the first floor landing. She lifted her skirts, revealing her worn and tattered undergarments. I felt a surge of disgust as she reached for me, but I had a job to do.

As she leaned in, I quickly grabbed her by the hair and slammed her head against the wall, knocking her senseless, and she slid down the wall. I remembered my uncle's words - 'If the creature is dead, there's no spray of blood.' With this in mind, I straddled her body and began to throttle the life out of her.

I could feel my blood-lust rising with every squeeze of my hands around her neck. Her feeble attempts to fight back only fueled my desire to end her miserable existence. As I felt her life slipping away, I took out my knife and began to stab her repeatedly in the throat and chest.

I lost track of how many times I stabbed her, but I could feel the adrenaline coursing through my veins. It was a feeling unlike any other, and I relished every moment of it. Satisfied that she was dead, I made my escape through the warren of dark lanes and passageways of the East End, and headed to my place of work.

As I walked through the deserted streets, I couldn't help but feel a sense of elation. I had done it - I had taken the life of that whore Martha Tabram, and got away with it. I reveled in the fact that I was above the law, that no one could stop me from satisfying my dark desires.

But as I reached my workplace, the reality of what I had done began to sink in. I had taken another human being's life without a second thought, and I didn't feel an ounce of shame or remorse. In fact, I felt empowered by the act.

I had been working all day, delivering meat, and running back and forth to the depot to replenish my cart. The sun blazed down on the East End streets, making the work even more taxing. But I was used to it, and so were my horses, Goliath and Sheba. I made sure to pause every now and then to quench their thirst and cool them down.

At seven o'clock, I returned to the depot, tired but satisfied with a day's work. I tended to my horses, rubbing them down and putting on their nose bags before making my way back home. As I walked, I noticed a young paper boy on the corner, shouting at the top of his lungs. 'Read all about it! Grizzly murder in Whitechapel! Woman found brutally murdered!'

My curiosity piqued, I approached the boy and bought a newspaper from him. As I read the headline, my heart beat faster and my hands began to shake. 'The Star, 7 August 1888. A Whitechapel horror,' it read. It went on to describe in gruesome detail the death of a woman in George buildings, where I had been just hours before.

My thoughts immediately turned to Martha Tabram, the woman I had killed just this morning. A smile crept upon my face as I thought about the blood and the life draining from her body.

But my inner voices began to scream within my head. They were angry that the newspaper report was not grand enough for such a monumental occasion.

'I was expecting a bigger write up!' I thought to myself angrily. This was my first kill, and I wanted to make sure the world knew it. 'I vow to mutilate all my future victims in such a way that the newspapers and all of London will talk about them,' I said to no one in particular.

I read on. The paper reported that no weapon was found near the victim's body, and the murderer had left no trace. I was beginning to realize that my killings were not being taken seriously. I would have to do something drastic to make the authorities and the newspapers pay attention. I wanted to put fear into the hearts of everyone in Whitechapel.

I arrived home and immediately poured myself a glass of Gin. I needed to calm my nerves and plan my next move. The atmosphere in my small home felt heavy and suffocating. The walls seemed to be closing in on me, and I could hear the screams of my inner voices growing louder.

I needed to release this anger and frustration, and there was only one way to do it.

16

Inspector Edmund Reid – from Beyond the Grave

My name is Edmund Reid, and I speak to you from beyond the grave. It has been many years since my passing, but the memories of my time as an inspector for the metropolitan police force, H division, still haunt me. Especially one particular case - the gruesome murder of Martha Tabram, a prostitute from the East End of London. It was the summer of 1888, a time when the Whitechapel district was a daily witness to poverty, crime, and the desperate struggle for survival.

It was on August 6th that the news of a woman's body found in George Buildings, Whitechapel, reached my office. I was immediately assigned to be the lead investigator in the case. As I made my way to the location, my mind was filled with various possibilities and suspects. However, nothing could have prepared me for the sight that awaited me.

The body of Martha Tabram was lying on the first floor landing, her pale lifeless form a stark contrast against the dirty brick walls of the building. She had been discovered by a Mr. John Saunders Reeve, who had been passing along the landing at around five in the morning. He immediately ran into the street and brought Constable Bennett, the local beat officer, to the scene. Bennett, on seeing the gruesome sight, quickly sent for the police doctor, Timothy Robert Killeen.

I vividly remember the feeling of unease that settled in me as I watched Doctor Killeen examine the body. His findings were just as disturbing as the sight before us. Martha had been brutally stabbed thirty-nine times all over her body, with nine of the wounds on her throat, five in her left lung, two in her right lung, one in her heart, five in her liver, two in her spleen, and six in her stomach. Her lower abdomen and genitals had also been attacked. She was lying on her back with her legs apart, her clothing pulled up to her middle. It was clear that her attacker had no mercy, and the brutality of the crime sent shivers down my spine.

The testimony of the residents and the doctor led us to believe that Martha had been killed between two and three-thirty in the morning. With this information, I immediately sent Constable Bennett to the Tower of London to see if he could identify a soldier who he had spotted standing in the street at around two in the morning. To our dismay, the soldier had an alibi - he had been drinking with his friends at a nearby pub. Despite this setback, we continued our investigations, questioning soldiers and local residents, but to no avail.

Her identity remained a mystery until her estranged husband came forward and identified her body on August 14th. It was a husband that she had left and remarried twice, but her troubled past and lifestyle had left her with no one to turn to for support.

The inquest into her death was held on August 23rd by Deputy Coroner George Collier, who concluded that Martha had been murdered by an unknown person or persons. The lack of any leads or suspects left us all feeling defeated. Despite our best efforts, we were unable to bring justice to Martha or her loved ones.

Years have passed since that fateful summer, and the identity of Martha's killer still remains a mystery. But as I look back on that investigation, I can't help but wonder if we missed something - a vital clue that could have led us to the perpetrator. But alas, I am no longer able to continue my investigation from beyond the grave.

Martha Tabram's death remains one of the cold cases of Whitechapel, and it still haunts me to this day. The East End of London in 1888 was a place of darkness and desperation, where the vulnerable fell prey to the merciless hands of evil. And in this case, it was Martha Tabram who became the unfortunate victim of the brutal streets of Whitechapel.

17
The Angel of Death

My name is Charles Allen Lechmere, and I speak to you from beyond the grave. It was the morning of August 31st 1888, and at three a.m I quietly let myself out of my front door and took my normal walk to my work at Pickford's. However, this morning was different. The voices in my head were screaming for another kill.

I had successfully killed Martha Tabram, and had been eagerly waiting for any news of the police getting close to finding her murderer. But nearly a month had passed and they were no closer. So, I decided to take matters into my own hands and go out again in search of my prey upon the dark streets of Whitechapel.

The night was dark, with very little moonlight. As I made my way along Doveton Street and into Cambridge Road, my footsteps echoed from the tall, dark buildings of the street. I continued on, turning down Buckfast Street and then into Darling Road, and Bath Street, before finally stopping in the shadows of an alleyway opposite a place called Bucks Row. I watched the local bobby PC Niel come down Bucks row, then turning the corner, he disappeared into the darkness of the streets. And I new that he wouldn't return for another half an hour, which gave me plenty of time for what I had to do. I had watched this particular area for many mornings now. I knew that this was where that bitch Polly Nichols plied her trade. And as luck would have it, it wasn't long before I saw her staggering down Darling Road, clearly drunk and leaning against a wall for support.

I casually emerged from my hiding place and walked across the road towards her. I knew that my kill would be easier because these foolish women always wanted money and would take their clients to a quiet, dark place, making it easy for me.

As I approached her, she said, 'Want a little excitement, deary?' I accepted her offer, and she took my arm, saying, 'Come down here, my dear. Little Polly will satisfy your every need.'

She led me down Bucks Row, a very dark street with only one lamp post at each end. The darkness of the street was so thick that you could only see a few feet in front of you. 'Come on, dear,' she said. 'Let's get comfortable here.'

I followed her, my heart racing with anticipation of the kill. She led me to a dark area in front of a stable yard. The perfect location for what I had in mind.

She leads me over to the two large black gates of the stable yard. And pulls me closer to her, the sight of her makes me feel sick in my stomach. She suddenly looks into my eyes, and as she lifts her skirts, she says, 'I know you, where have I seen you before?'

I don't answer her question. I can sense her curiosity, her attempt to figure out why I seem familiar. But I can't reveal who I truly am, not even to a lowly prostitute like her.

She looks at me for a few seconds longer, then says, 'Never mind, I must be mistaken.' Her words bring a sense of relief to me, but also a wave of anger.

How dare she think she knows me. I am untouchable, a powerful man who has committed a heinous crime without getting caught.

'You shall know me by another name before this night is through,' I answer, my voice deep and menacing. I am the angel of death, come to take your soul.

She looks at me once more, and a look of terror crosses her face, and she lets out a scream. But just at that moment, a late-night goods train comes thundering along the railway line that passes close to the road. Its whistle blowing and the clatter of its wheels drowning the whore's cry for help.

I take advantage of the noise and hit her in the face. She falls to the ground, and I grab her by the throat, and start to throttle her. Very soon she is lying at my feet, and the life has left her, and I take my knife from beneath my apron. I then cut twice deeply into her throat.

But I am not done yet. The blood lust rises within me, and I proceed to mutilate her body in many ways. I cut into her abdomen, her internal organs spilling out, her blood mixing with the filth of the street.

But my moment of pleasure is interrupted by the sound of heavy footsteps approaching from the end of the street. And panic sets in as I quickly wipe the blood from my hands and pull the whore's clothing down to cover what I have done.

Many thoughts race through my mind. Do I kill him, or do I run away? No, I think to myself, if I run, the man will chase after me, crying out for help, and that would bring every copper within hearing distance to this place. No, that would be a silly mistake on my part. So I decide to stand my ground, and make it appear that I have just discovered the body.

I stand back from the whore's body, and wait until the man draws closer. Then I go to stop him on the other side of the street. He sees me and stops a few feet away. I call out to him, look what I've found, there's a woman over here, and we both walk over to the body. And we examine it.

I touch her face, then her hands, and tell the man they are cold. 'I think she is dead,' I say.

The man then seems uncertain, then says, 'I think she may be drunk, and unconscious.' He reaches out and feels her heart. 'I think there is some life still in her but only just,' he says, looking at me for help. Do you think we should prop her up against the gates?

But I couldn't bring myself to touch her. I knew that once I helped move her, the full extent of her injuries would be revealed.

Without thinking, I took out my pocket watch and checked the time. It was nearly four o'clock. 'I shall get it in the neck if I arrive late at the depot,' I said, more to myself than to the man.

He replied that he also needed to be at work soon.

We decided to make our way together and alert the authorities about the woman in Bucks Row. As we walked, I found out that his name was Robert Paul and he worked as a carman, just like myself. I didn't tell him my name for obvious reasons.

The streets were dark and quiet, except for the occasional drunken shout or cry for help. The only source of light was the dim street lamps, casting eerie shadows on the deserted streets. We walked in silence, both consumed by our own thoughts and fears.

As we turned into Hanbury Street, we noticed a policeman at the corner of Bakers Row. He was on 'knocking up' duty, a common practice in Whitechapel where officers would knock on doors to wake people up for work.

I told Robert to stay on the other side of the street as I approached the officer. 'Excuse me, officer,' I said, trying to sound as calm as possible. 'There's a woman lying in Bucks Row, and a policeman is with her asking for assistance. She looks either dead or drunk, but I believe she may be dead.'

The policeman thanked me and quickly made his way towards Bucks Row, where we had originally come from. I purposely added the detail about the other policeman, knowing that PC Neal, the officer on duty, would have already found the woman's body by now.

Relieved that I had got away with my lies, we continued our journey to work. But just seconds after we started walking, we heard a sound that sent chills down my spine - a police whistle. I knew I was right about PC Neal finding Polly Nichols' body.

I couldn't believe it - I had just killed a woman, and had fooled everyone about discovering her body.

As we reached our destinations, we quickly parted ways, not wanting to be associated with each other any longer.

18

Frederick Abberline – from Beyond the Grave

My name is Frederick Abberline, and I speak to you from beyond the grave. In August 1888, I was called from my usual place of work at Scotland Yard to investigate a series of gruesome murders that had taken place in Whitechapel. I remember the details vividly, even after all these years.

I was a detective inspector at the time and had been assigned to the notorious 'H' Division, responsible for policing London's East End, a place known for its poverty, crime, and dark secrets. But nothing could have prepared me for the horrors I was about to uncover.

On arriving at the murder site in Bucks Row, I found two police officers standing near the body of a woman that was laying in front of the two black gates of a stable yard. PC Neil and PC Thain were the first responders, and the police doctor, Dr. Llewellyn, was already examining the body when I arrived.

The victim's body was laying upon the ground, with a black bonnet laying near her left hand. I could see that the poor woman had been brutally attacked.

The deep cuts in her throat weren't seen until the body was moved, and the doctor confirmed that she had been dead for about 30 minutes.

I asked PC Neil how he had come across the body, and he told me that he had seen something lying in the dark by the gates, and upon closer inspection with his torch, he found it to be a body. PC Thain had heard PC Neil calling for assistance from his beat, which passed the other end of Bucks Row, and had come to assist.

Soon after, another constable arrived, a PC Mizen sir. He informed me that he had heard I needed assistance in Bucks row, from two men who were on their way to work. I thanked PC Neil for his information and asked if there were any clues. PC Neil replied that he had searched the area but found nothing.

As more police officers arrived, I directed them to keep the growing crowd back and clear the street if possible. PC Mizen had also brought a hand cart from the mortuary, and we carefully lifted the body onto it to take it away.

But it was when we lifted the body that the full extent of the injuries to the woman's throat became apparent. The maniac who had made the cuts into her throat, had cut so deep that it went right back to the vertebral column. It was a sight that would haunt me for the rest of my days.

My investigation had officially begun. I knew that I had to discover the identity of this poor woman and bring her killer to justice. And little did I know that this would be the start of a string of murders that would grip London and the rest of the world with fear and horror.

When I arrived at the mortuary, the atmosphere was grim. The stench of death hung heavy in the air as I made my way inside. As an inspector for the Metropolitan Police, I have seen my fair share of horrific crime scenes, but something about this one felt different. Perhaps it was the fact that the victim was a woman, or the sheer brutality of the crime, but I couldn't shake off the feeling of unease.

Doctor Llewellyn, the medical examiner, greeted me upon my arrival. He was a stout man with a gruff demeanor, but I had worked with him before and knew him to be a skilled doctor. I followed him to the examination room, where the body lay upon the cold metal table.

'Inspector Abberline, good to see you,' Doctor Llewellyn said, nodding his head in greeting. 'I have just completed my examination of the body.'

'What have you found?' I asked, eager to hear his findings.

We have had a positive identification, said the doctor. Her name is Mary Ann Nichols. But on the street she was known as Polly.

'It's a nasty business,' he replied, shaking his head. 'The list of her injuries is long.'

He proceeded to describe the brutal murder in detail, and I grimaced at each word. 'Both sides of her face are bruised, as if she was hit, either by a fist or the pressure of a thumb before the wounds were inflicted upon her throat. The knife wounds run from left to right. One of these wounds was eight inches long, the other four inches, both reaching the vertebral column.'

I clenched my fist at the sheer brutality of the attack. 'Her vagina has been stabbed twice, and her abdomen has been mutilated, with one deep jagged wound two to three inches from her left side, causing her bowel to protrude through the wound. Two or three cuts to the right side of her body, also made with the same weapon. Each cut has been made with a violent downward thrusting manner.'

I had to look away from the body, feeling sick at the thought of someone inflicting such pain and suffering on another human being. 'What about the weapon used?'

'I cannot say for sure, but it appears to be a sharp, single-edged knife, around six to eight inches in length,' Doctor Llewellyn replied. 'And from the precision and depth of the wounds, I believe that the murderer has some sort of anatomical knowledge. Although there are no organs missing, he may have been disturbed in the act.'

I nodded, taking in the information. 'How long do you think the attack lasted?'

'I estimate that the wounds would have taken around four to five minutes to complete,' the doctor said. 'And I was also surprised at the lack of blood at the crime scene. It leads me to believe that she was already dead before he butchered her. Very little blood would flow if she was dead before being cut up.'

I thanked the doctor for his thorough examination and left the mortuary, deep in thought. It was clear that we were dealing with a disturbed and dangerous individual. But what motive could they have had for such a heinous crime?

As I walked the dark streets of the East End, my mind kept returning to the details of the murder. It was clear that the culprit was someone with knowledge of anatomy, perhaps a doctor or a surgeon, or maybe a butcher or slaughterman. But who could it be?

Returning to the police station after another grueling day, I knew that we needed to take a different approach. I immediately called for a meeting with all the officers involved in the case.

As they gathered in my office, I briefed them on the latest information I had received from the mortuary. Doctor Llewellyn had observed some peculiarities in the crime scene and the wounds on the victims, leading us to believe that the killer had some knowledge of anatomy.

'So gentlemen,' I began, looking around at the assembled officers, 'we are looking for a man who has some knowledge of anatomy, or so we think.'

I could see the confusion and concern on their faces. This was a daunting task, but we had to try something new if we were to catch this killer before he struck again.

'My first order of business is to have all of you interview all the doctors and surgeons in an area of five miles from the murder site. We need to gather as much information as possible,' I explained, hoping to instill a sense of urgency in their actions.

I continued, 'Also, we need to interview all the butchers, slaughtermen, and horse slaughterers in the Whitechapel area. It may seem like a tedious task, but we cannot afford to overlook any potential suspects.

'And finally,' I said, pausing for emphasis, 'I want some of you to go to every door in Whitechapel and Spitalfields, interview every man and woman in every house. We need to leave no stone unturned, gentlemen.'

My colleagues nodded in understanding, their faces grim. We all knew that time was of the essence. This killer had already claimed a possible four lives and we couldn't let him take any more.

'But what type of man are we looking for?' asked one of the constables, breaking the silence.

I took a deep breath before replying, 'He will be a man that blends in with the crowd, someone we wouldn't suspect. He is a man who can walk the streets unseen to the average person.'

'You say a man sir,' another constable spoke up, 'but couldn't it be a woman?'

I couldn't help but scoff at the thought. 'I have seen what this person can do to his victims, constable.

Trust me, no woman would have the strength to hold the victim down and inflict the injuries I have seen. No, we are definitely looking for a man.'

After answering their questions and clarifying some details, the meeting came to an end and the search began.

Every door was knocked in the Whitechapel area, and every doctor, surgeon, butcher, and slaughterer was questioned. Over two thousand people were interviewed, with no results.

But we didn't stop there. We extended the search to every corner of London, known for its poverty and crime. We visited the many doss houses, hoping to find someone who may have seen or heard something that could give us a lead.

The long days turned into weeks, But still, we had no solid leads or suspects.

As time passed, the people of the East End began to live in terror of the fiend that stalked the streets of Whitechapel, I secretly thought he would stop his mad killing spree. But I knew better, I knew that this killer was still out there, watching and waiting for his next victim.

But for me and the rest of the police department, this case would never be forgotten. It would be etched in our minds and hearts forever, a constant reminder of the evil that lurked in the shadows of the East End streets of London in the year 1888.

19

The Inquest of Polly Nichols

My name is Charles Allen Lechmere, and I speak to you from beyond the grave. I was once a resident of Whitechapel, a quiet and unassuming man by day, but a different man entirely by night. I was a skilled carman, and I used this cover to navigate the dark and dangerous streets of Whitechapel.

It was the year 1888 when the newspapers were filled with news of the gruesome murders of prostitutes in Whitechapel. I followed these stories with great interest, for I knew that they were my handiwork. Yet, I remained calm and collected, knowing that my identity was safe for the time being.

But then, one day, as I perused the newspaper, I came across an article that caught my attention. It was about the inquest into the death of one of my victim's, the whore Polly Nichols. The second day of the inquest hearing was to be held at the Working Lads Institute in Whitechapel Road, on Saturday, 3rd September. I was in two minds whether to attend or not. After all, nobody knew my name or my address. But then, I thought, what if the man who had almost caught me in the act of murdering the whore should attend the inquest? He knew I was a carman, and if he disclosed this information, it wouldn't be long before the coppers started asking questions at every depot in the East End.

But my morbid curiosity got the better of me. I wanted to know what was being said about my victims, about my crimes. So, I decided to attend the inquest, to hear for myself what was being said. I also wanted to testify, but not before knowing what the other witnesses had to say.

On the day of the inquest, I made my way to the large brick building that was the Working Lads Institute. As I entered the building, I could see that it was crowded. The first person I spotted was Robert Paul, the carman who had almost stumbled upon me while I was committing my heinous act. He immediately recognized me and gave me a nod of recognition. I simply nodded back and quickly lost myself in the crowd. I didn't want to be associated with a potential witness.

Soon, the doors to the hall were opened, and we were all summoned to enter. Paul made his way to the front, while I took a seat towards the back. The hall was called to silence and a door opened, revealing the coroner for Middlesex, Wynne Edwin Baxter. He took his seat at a long table at the front of the hall, and the jury was sworn in.

'We are here to look into the death of one Mary Anne Nichols,' declared the coroner. 'She was found dead on 31st August 1888, in Buck's Row, Whitechapel. All those who wish to testify of their own free will, please raise your hands. One of my colleagues will then come and take your names.'

I saw Paul raise his hand, and I followed suit. As I sat in the court house, listening to the inquest of Polly Nichols, I couldn't help but smile to myself. They were never going to catch me. I was too clever, too cunning. I was the killer, but no one knew it yet. They didn't even have a name for me, but they would soon enough.

The first witness to be called was a police inspector named John Spratling. I watched as he took the stand, and I couldn't help but feel a sense of satisfaction. He testified that he had first heard about the body of a woman in Bucks row at 4:30 a.m., by which time the body had already been moved to the mortuary. Spratling also confirmed that only PC Neil's beat required him to walk through Bucks row.

The next witness was a police constable named Mizen. He had been the one I told about the body on my way to work. Mizen told the court that he had been informed by a carman about the body in Bucks row. He had thought that the carman had said that another policeman was already with the body. Upon his arrival, he had found PC Neil standing by the body, and Neil had told him to fetch a cart from the mortuary and inform Doctor Llewellyn of the discovery.

The coroner then asked Mizen if the carman was present in the court. Mizen pointed directly at me and said, 'He is the man sitting two rows from the back.' I sat there calmly, knowing there was no way they could ever suspect me. I was just another innocent bystander, caught up in the chaos of the East End.

As I was called to the stand, I couldn't help but feel a thrill run through my body. I was a part of the investigation, and they didn't even know it. I stood up and made my way to the stand, wearing my work clothes and my long apron, stained with the blood of my work and my victims. It was the perfect disguise.

The coroner asked me to state my name and address for the court. I confidently lied, 'My name is Charles Cross. I live at 22 Doveton Street, Whitechapel.'

He then asked me to tell the court about the morning of the 31st of August, the day I had killed Polly Nichols. I lied again, telling them a carefully crafted story that would lead them away from the truth.

'I left my home at my usual time of 3:30 a.m.,' I said. 'And as I was walking down Bucks row, I saw something lying on the other side of the road. At first, I thought it was a tarpaulin, but as I came closer, I discovered it was the body of a woman. A little while later, another carman arrived, and together we examined the body.'

The coroner looked at me intently. 'And did you see anyone else around at the time?'

I shook my head. 'No sir, it was just the two of us. And did you tell PC Mizen that there was a policeman who was with the body in Bucks Row, asked the coroner. No sir, I lied. I couldn't have said that there was a policeman in Bucks Row, because there was only the two of us at the scene of the murder. and I think if you ask the carman who was with me, he will tell you the same.

The coroner nodded and thanked me for my testimony. I took my seat again, feeling pleased with myself. No one suspected a thing. I was just a helpful witness, aiding in the investigation.

Robert Paul was then called to the stand. He gave his side of the story, which was much the same as mine.

As the inquest continued, I listened to the testimonies of other witnesses, always making sure to remember every detail they shared. I wanted to make sure no one else could catch me. I was always one step ahead.

As the hearing came to an end, the verdict of death by person or persons unknown was given, and the inquest came to an end.

But as the days passed and the investigation continued, the police still had no leads. They questioned many people in the Whitechapel area, but none of them had any useful information. They were getting desperate, and I could see it in their faces. They knew there was a killer on the loose, but they couldn't find him.

I kept my routine, continuing to go to work every day and keeping a low profile. I even went to the funerals of my victims, just to see the devastation I had caused. It was a sick pleasure, but I couldn't resist.

Very soon they will be burying another whore. And that time will be coming very soon, I said to myself with a smile.

Over the next few days, I began my search for my next victim. I roamed the streets of Whitechapel, keeping my eyes peeled for my potential target, But as the days went by, I couldn't seem to find the one I was looking for. Annie Chapman, the whore. I longed to make her my next prey.

Just when I was about to give up, I stumbled upon a young boy named Albie Tatterly. He was a street urchin, with dirty clothes and a mischievous glint in his eyes. I approached him, and in his thick cockney accent, he said, 'Wot ya lookin for, guvn'a?'

I told him that I was searching for a woman called Annie Chapman, and I needed someone who could help me find her. The boy's eyes lit up, and with a grin, he said, 'I'll find the ladies whereabouts by this evenin, guvna.'

I promised him sixpence if he could find her, to which he eagerly accepted. He then asked where he could find me with the information, and I told him I would meet him near the Duke of Wellington pub at seven thirty.

As the day went on, I tried to keep myself busy, but my mind was consumed with the thought of finally finding Annie Chapman. At seven o'clock, I told my wife that I was going for a drink, and she kissed me on the cheek, unaware of my true intentions.

As I approached the Duke of Wellington pub, I saw Albie leaning against the wall, just as he had promised. He gave me a cheeky smile as I approached, and in a low voice, he said, 'I found out what ya wanted to know.'

I motioned for him to follow me to a quieter place, away from the prying ears of the pub. I didn't want anyone to suspect my involvement with the dark deeds I was planning. I took out the sixpence and showed it to him, making sure he knew that I was a man of my word.

'Tell me, what have you found out?' I asked, eager for any information.

The boy's face lit up, and he said, 'I found 'er, guvna! She lives at a lodgin 'owse on Dorset Street. 'Tis called Crossinghams lodgin 'owse, number 35.'

I couldn't contain my excitement. Albie had done well, and I couldn't wait to finally lay my hands on Annie Chapman. I thanked him and passed the coin over, reminding him to keep his mouth shut about our conversation.

'No need to worry, mista. Albie Tatterly knows when ta keep is gob shut,' he said with a sly grin.

I watched as he skipped away, flipping the coin in the air. But my mind was already focused on Annie Chapman. I had found her, and now it was only a matter of time until I had her in my grasp.

Over the next few days, I made sure to keep a close eye on Annie. I followed her every move, making sure she was alone and in a secluded place. And then, the day finally came.

(CHAPTER TWENTY) FREDERICK ABBERLINE FROM BEYOND THE GRAVE.

My name is Frederick Abberline, and I speak to you from beyond the grave. As I reflect back on the start of our investigation into the murders of Martha Tabram and Polly Nichols, I am reminded of the chaos and fear that consumed London in the year 1888. It was a time like no other, when the streets were stained with blood and the air was filled with a sense of dread.

It all began with the discovery of Martha Tabram's lifeless body on the early morning of August 7th.

Her throat had been brutally slit and her body had been stabbed multiple times. It was a gruesome sight, one that haunted me even in my dreams. As the lead inspector in the case, I knew that this was no ordinary murder. There was something sinister lurking in the shadows of London, and it was my duty to uncover the truth.

The investigation began in full force, and over 2000 people were brought in for questioning.

We followed up on 300 lines of enquiry, but no solid leads emerged. It seemed like the killer had vanished into thin air, leaving us with nothing but a trail of blood and terror. But I was determined to crack the case. I knew that our only hope was to gather as much evidence as possible. And that's why I decided to change the way we handled witness statements.

I made it a rule that all witness statements had to be written in the words of the witness, without any alterations. The original words had to be crossed out in case of any errors, but should still be visible, and each page was to be signed by both the witness and the interviewing officer. This helped us to maintain the integrity of the statements and prevented any discrepancies from arising. It was a major breakthrough in our investigation, and it led us to a number of potential suspects.

Around the same time, the newspapers started to publish exaggerated stories about the murders. One paper even claimed that a man known as 'Leather Apron', a shoemaker, was the culprit behind the gruesome killings. This sparked a wave of anti-Semitic demonstrations and riots in the streets of London. Innocent people were being targeted, and it was clear that these rumors were damaging the progress of our investigation.

Following the newspaper report, we managed to track down a Polish Jew named John Pizer, a man who fitted the description of 'Leather Apron'. He had gone into hiding at the house of a family member, fearing for his life. We arrested him and brought him in for questioning, but it turned out that he had a solid alibi for the nights of the murders. We had to let him go, but the damage had already been done. The newspapers had created a frenzy, leading to innocent people being wrongly accused.

The media's irresponsibility not only caused chaos in the streets, but also led our investigation to a dead end. Suspects were now going into hiding, making it even more difficult for us to catch the real killer. But despite these setbacks, I was determined to continue with the investigation. I refused to let the fear and hatred consume our efforts.

As the weeks went by, the body count continued to rise. The streets were filled with prostitutes, and the killer seemed to have a specific target - women who were destitute and vulnerable. It was a daunting task, trying to catch someone who was able to evade the police at every turn. But we carried on, determined to bring justice to the victims and their families.

Despite our persistence, we could not seem to get any closer to catching the maniac that was terrorizing the streets of London. The whole city was gripped with fear, and it seemed like the killer was always one step ahead of us. The days turned into weeks, but the killer remained at large.

Even in death, I cannot help but wonder - could we have done more? Could we have caught the killer before he claimed more innocent lives? It is a question that will haunt me for eternity. And as I watch from beyond the grave, I can only hope that one day, the true identity of the murderer will be revealed and the families of his victims will find the closure they deserve. Until then, I remain as a shadow, forever linked to the infamous murders of London's East End.

21

Charles Allen Lechmere – from Beyond the Grave. The Murder of Annie Chapman

My name is Charles Allen Lechmere, and I speak to you from beyond the grave. My story is one of darkness, bloodshed, and a thirst for power. I was never caught for my crimes, and I feel no remorse for what I have done. I am writing this in hopes that my twisted tale will be remembered forever.

It all started in the year 1888, in the dark streets of East End London. The poverty was suffocating, and the stench of misery lingered in the air. It was the perfect setting for my dark desires to thrive. I had found the whereabouts of the whore Annie Chapman, and she would be my next victim.

At 3 a.m. on Monday morning, I made my way through the eerie streets, my destination - Dorset Street. I hid in the shadows of a brewery arch and waited. This became my routine for the next few days. I observed the movements of the local bobbies and the activities of everyone who passed through Dorset Street at that ungodly hour.

Annie appeared many times, but it was around 4 to 4:30 a.m. that she would walk the streets in search of clients. I knew this was the perfect time to strike. I would have to make some excuses for my late arrival at work, but that was a small price to pay for the satisfaction I would gain. My boss at Pickford's, where I worked, trusted me and never questioned my excuses.

With my plan in place, I made up my mind that Saturday night would be Annie Chapman's last. I informed my boss that my mother was unwell, and I would be late for work on Saturday. He expressed his concern and wished her a speedy recovery, oblivious to my true intentions.

On Saturday, 8th September 1888, I left my home at 3 a.m. and made my way to Dorset Street. I hid in the shadows, waiting for my prey to appear. At 4:45 a.m., I saw Annie walking from one of the pubs. She called out to me, 'Want a bit of fun, love? Only cost ya fourpence.' I accepted her offer, and she led me to a dark backyard.

In that moment, my bloodlust rose like a fiery inferno. I grabbed her neck and throttled her, her screams becoming muffled as she struggled to breathe. She fell to the ground, and I unleashed my knife, tearing open her body with no mercy. The satisfaction I felt was indescribable. I had fulfilled my desires, and no one could stop me.

As I stood there, admiring my handiwork, I couldn't help but feel a sense of power and control. I was untouchable, invincible. No one could stop me. I took pleasure in taunting the authorities, leaving my mark on the bodies of my victims. I reveled in the fear and chaos I caused in the streets of Whitechapel.

I continued to hunt and kill, my thirst for power growing with each victim. The streets of the East End London were my playground, and the bobbies were my puppets, unable to catch me as I slipped through their fingers.

As I tell my bloody story, I am no longer of this world. But my legacy lives on. My story will be told for generations to come. And in my death, I found ultimate satisfaction, for I had fulfilled my sinister desires and left a mark on history that can never be erased.

22

Edward Swanson
– from Beyond the Grave

My name is Edward Swanson, and I speak to you from beyond the grave. I was the chief police inspector in charge of the investigation into the murder of one Annie Chapman, a prostitute who had been found in the backyard of 29 Hanbury street Whitechapel. It was 1888 and I was working tirelessly to solve this gruesome case.

I had attended the murder scene, and had found that the poor woman had had her throat cut, and her body had been terribly mutilated. She layed in the corner of the yard upon her back with her legs open, the sight was one of the worst murder scenes I have ever attended. It was clear that the perpetrator had a deep hatred towards women, and the way he had mutilated Annie's body showed the true extent of his rage.

Upon the bodies removal to the mortuary, I had my men search the yard for clues. But all we found was two farthing coins which lay next to the body. The following morning, I made my way to the mortuary, to find out more of the poor woman's injuries. On my arrival, I found Dr. George Baxter Phillips examining the body. He greeted me with a sad smile.

I asked him what he had found, and he replied with a heavy heart, 'Well inspector, the throat has been cut twice from left to right, the cuts are so deep that they have scored the vertebral column. She has been disemboweled. When I examined her body at the murder scene, her intestines had been pulled out, and placed over her left shoulder. Part of her stomach has been removed, plus her small intestine had been removed and placed over her right shoulder. Also, part of her uterus and bladder are missing.' I took in his words with a heavy heart, knowing that we were dealing with a brutal and calculating killer.

As Dr. Phillips continued his examination, he remarked, 'I think we are dealing with someone who has a definite knowledge of anatomy. The way the organs have been removed and placed shows that the killer had a certain level of skill.' I thanked him for his assessment, but I couldn't help but feel anger and disgust towards the killer. How could someone do such a horrific thing to another human being?

Leaving the mortuary, I made my way back to the police station. With no leads or suspects, we had to rely on witness statements and anyone who may have seen or heard something on the night of the murder. We spoke to many people who knew Annie Chapman, but no one seemed to have any useful information.

As days turned into weeks and weeks turned into months, the case remained unsolved. I went to bed every night with the frustration and guilt of not being able to catch the killer. The streets of Whitechapel were filled with fear and the women of the night were living in constant terror, not knowing if they would be the next victim of this madman. I remember it all too clearly, the year was 1888 and Whitechapel was a place filled with terror and fear. It seemed like every corner held a new danger and every shadow hid a monstrous figure.

The streets were dark and the atmosphere heavy with the scent of fear. People were cautious, constantly on guard, and for good reason.

For a number of days, there was no sign of the Whitechapel murderer. Not one murder had been committed since that of Annie Chapman. Secretly, everyone within Whitechapel hoped that that was the end of this maniac's reign of terror, but I knew that it was only a matter of time before he struck once more. The days passed with no sign of the Whitechapel murderers evil crimes, and everyone gave a sigh of relief. The days turned into weeks, but the investigation went on.

Until one day, upon the 27th of September, I received a call from a man named Mr. Frank Miles who worked at the Central news agency. He informed me that he had received a strange letter in the post that morning, and he thought I should read it. I asked him to come to my office, and he arrived promptly at 10 a.m. I showed him to a seat and he passed the letter to me.

It was written in red ink and it sent chills down my spine as I read the words.

'Dear Boss, I keep hearing the police have caught me but they won't fix me yet. I have laughed when they look so clever and talk about being on the right track. That joke about Leather Apron gave me real fits. I am down on whores and I shan't quit ripping them till I do get buckled. Grand work the last job was. I gave the lady no time to squeal. I love my work and want to start again. You will soon hear of me with my funny little games. I saved some of the proper red stuff in a ginger beer bottle over the last job to write with but it went thick like glue and I can't use it. Red ink is fit enough I hope ha ha. The next job I do I shall clip the lady's ears off and send them to the police officers just for jolly, wouldn't you? Keep this letter back till I do a bit more work, then give it out straight. My knife's so nice and sharp I want to get to work right away if I get the chance. Good luck. Yours truly, Jack the Ripper. P.S. Wasn't good enough to post this before I got all the red ink off my hands, curse it. No luck yet. They say I'm a doctor now, ha ha.'

I sat for some minutes in silence, before I looked up at Mr. Miles. Thank you for bringing this letter to me so promptly I said. But we have had hundreds of similar letters, all reporting that the writer is the Whitechapel murderer. But there is something about this particular letter that makes me think somehow this could be from the maniac himself. Do you mind if I keep the letter, maybe someone may recognise the hand writing. Mr. Miles said yes, and I rose from my chair and saw the gentleman out.

Over the next few days, we asked the many newspapers of London to print the letter on their front pages, in the hope that someone might come forward with information.

The handwriting was crude and the words were sinister. The thought of this madman roaming the streets, waiting to strike again, sent shivers down my spine. I knew that it was only a matter of time before he claimed another victim.

Immediately, I sent for reinforcements and the investigation team launched into action once more. We scoured the streets, questioning individuals and keeping a close eye on any suspicious behavior. But the days continued to pass without any sign of the elusive killer.

The publication of the murder caused mass hysteria in the streets of Whitechapel as people feared for their lives. And the media frenzy only made things worse. False leads and accusations flooded in, but we still had no concrete evidence or suspects.

Time went on and more murders occurred. Each one more gruesome and horrifying than the last. We were chasing a shadow, a ghost who seemed to always be one step ahead of us.

23

Charles Allen Lechmere – from Beyond the Grave. The Double Event

My name is Charles Allen Lechmere, and I speak to you from beyond the grave. As I sit here in the afterlife, reflecting on my life and my actions, I cannot help but think about the events that led me to become known as the infamous Jack the Ripper. It all started on a busy evening in Whitechapel Road, back in 1888.

After a long day of work, I made my way to the Blind Beggar pub. I walked through the bustling street, observing the people going about their daily routines. Some were rushing to get home, while others were leisurely strolling, enjoying the warm evening air.

Finally, I arrived at the pub and made my way to the bar. I ordered a pint of Banks mild and took a seat in the corner, taking my newspaper out from under my arm. As I sipped my drink, I perused the newspaper and came across a peculiar letter on the front page, written in red ink.

At first, I couldn't believe my eyes. Someone had written this letter and sent it to the Central News Agency, claiming to be the Whitechapel murderer. As I read on, I couldn't help but chuckle to myself. It was quite amusing to see someone take the blame for my actions.

But as I continued reading, my amusement turned to curiosity. The letter described my dark nature and my crimes perfectly. And most importantly, it gave me a name - Jack the Ripper. I couldn't help but think that it had a good ring to it.

As I sat there, pondering on the letter, I realized that this person had unknowingly given me an advantage. Not only did they give me a name, but they also informed the police about what they planned to do with the next victim - clip her ears and send them to the police.

I couldn't resist a wicked smile as I thought to myself that this was a stroke of luck. The police would undoubtedly think that the letter was written by the true murderer, and that would lead them on a false trail of investigation. Beneath the letter, I noticed it was written that anyone who recognized the handwriting or had any information should contact the police.

I couldn't believe my luck. This person had essentially done my work for me. I decided then and there that my next victim, Elizabeth Stride, would be the one to have her ears clipped and her body mutilated beyond recognition.

With a sly grin, I finished my pint of beer, tucked my newspaper under my arm, and left the pub. As I walked down Whitechapel Road, I couldn't shake off the excitement of the events to come. In just a few days, on Sunday, September 30th, Long Liz Stride would meet her end by the hands of Jack the Ripper.

It was the evening of Saturday, September 29th. I had told my wife that I was going to visit my mother in Cable Street and would be spending the night with her. My wife kissed me goodbye and told me to give her love to my mother. It was all part of my plan. I needed an alibi for what I was about to do.

My mother and stepfather went to bed at nine o'clock. I knew this because I had stayed with them before. They were early sleepers and with a little help from some Laudanum, they would sleep like babies until the next morning. It was not something I enjoyed doing to my mother and stepfather, but I needed to make sure they were sound asleep before I left the house.

As the night progressed, I made my way to the kitchen and put a kettle on the range. Once it was boiling, I added a few drops of Laudanum to the pot. My mother and stepfather drank their tea and soon mentioned how sleepy they were feeling. I offered to stay with them and make sure they were comfortable, but they insisted that I go to bed.

So, I settled myself on the sofa next to the fire and waited. I waited until I was certain that my mother and stepfather were sleeping soundly, and then I quietly crept out of the house and into the streets of Whitechapel.

My destination was Berner Street. I knew this was where that whore Elizabeth Stride would be. This was it, this was the night I would make her mine. I had been watching her for a while now, studying her every move.

When I reached Burner Street I stood in the shadows, waiting for her. And not long after, I saw her walking down the street. I watched as she stopped at the corner of Burner Street and leaned against the wall. My heart began to race, this was it. I was just about to make my move when a man in a long black coat approached her. I felt a surge of anger, but I waited. Very soon, the man left and the whore continued walking down the street.

I followed her, keeping my distance, watching her as she made her way towards a stable yard. She stopped near the entrance for a minute or two, probably looking for a place to pee.

But I was not interested in her bathroom habits. I was only interested in taking her life.

I slowly made my way towards her, making sure she didn't hear me. She was standing with her back to me, unaware of my presence. I took a deep breath and approached her from behind. I was so close now, I could hear her breathing.

Without a second thought, I wrapped my hands around her neck, cutting off her air supply. She struggled and tried to scream, but I only tightened my hold on her. Suddenly her body went limp, and I dragged her into the darkness of the stable yard. Then taking my knife I cut deeply into her throat. Lifting her skirts I then prepared to mutilate her body beyond recognition. But just as I was about to do the deed, I heard the sound of a horse drawn vehicle approaching from down the street, I stopped my work and listened. The sound of the horses' hooves drew closer, until they suddenly stopped just the other side of the large double gates of the stable yard. I made myself quickly to the gate that had been left partially open, and hid behind it. Very soon the gates were pushed open, and the owner of the two wheeled cart drove into the yard. He jumped down from the driving seat, and went to unharness the horse. But suddenly he saw the dark shape of the whores body laying in the yard's corner, and goes over to see what is the matter. He then bends over the body, and upon feeling her pulse, runs from the yard for help. I immediately come from my hiding place, and making sure the street is quiet, I flee the murder scene, and disappear like a ghost into the alleyways of Whitechapel.

As I made my way through the dark and dirty alleyways, my inner voices were screaming at me, urging me to continue my bloodthirsty rampage. I tried to fight them off, but my hatred for all whores was overwhelming. They were the lowest of the low, unclean and sinful in the eyes of God.

But as I ran, the adrenaline began to wear off and I slowed my pace. I couldn't risk being seen by a copper, for he would surely take me in for questioning. My anger boiled within me, furious that I had been unable to fulfill my desire to mutilate Stride's body. I needed to kill once more before I could satisfy the voices in my head.

I headed west, towards St. Botolph's Church, also known as the 'prostitutes' church' due to the many whore bitches who would circle the building, trying to pick up clients. I was certain I would find my next victim there, and I had my sights set on a particular whore, Catherine Eddowes.

As I arrived at the church, I hid in the shadows and peered out at the women circling the yard. But there were not many of them tonight, and I began to feel a twinge of disappointment. I waited for what felt like an eternity, until I finally spotted Eddowes. She stood by the gates of the church, looking around for any potential clients. It looked like she hadn't had much luck picking up any business tonight.

After a few minutes, she bid farewell to one of the other whores and began to make her way down the street. I trailed behind her, always keeping to the shadows. She walked slowly, as if she were tired or perhaps disappointed at her lack of clients. I followed her through the dark and dingy streets, until she finally turned down a narrow alleyway.

I continued to follow her, keeping my distance so as not to raise any suspicions. After a few turns, she came to a stop in Mitre Square. I watched from the shadows as she looked around, seemingly unaware of my presence. I waited for a moment, then slowly made my way towards her, my knife at the ready.

24

Frederick Abberline – from Beyond the Grave

My name is Frederick Abberline, and I speak to you from beyond the grave. In the early hours of Sunday 30th September 1888, I was woken by a call from my colleague, Chief Inspector Donald Swanson. He informed me of yet another murder that had taken place in Whitechapel. Without hesitation, I washed and dressed, and was at the murder scene within half an hour.

As I arrived, I found Inspector Swanson at the scene with a number of police constables. Also present was Doctor Frederick William Blackwell, who was bent over the body of a woman lying on her back in the far corner of the yard.

Swanson came over to greet me as soon as I arrived. 'Poor woman's had her throat cut from ear to ear,' he said, shaking his head. 'But there are no mutilations to the body. Somehow, I don't think this is our man, Jack the Ripper.'

I stood there, thinking for a moment before responding. 'What makes you think that, sir?' I asked.

'Well, all the other victims were badly mutilated,' Swanson replied, gesturing towards the body. 'This one looks like she was only killed for her money.'

I followed Swanson over to the body and looked down upon the horrific sight. After a few moments of contemplation, I spoke again. 'But what if the murderer was disturbed in the act? He might not have had enough time to complete the mutilations.' I suggested.

Swanson nodded thoughtfully. 'That's a possibility,' he conceded. 'If that's the case, then I don't think he would have been satisfied with just one kill. He would have gone to find another victim, to fulfill his blood lust.' I replied.

I furrowed my brow, deep in thought. 'No, I think we'll be hearing from him again tonight,' I predicted.

Just as I spoke those words, a police constable from the City of London Police entered the yard and informed us of another murder on their patch. Swanson and I exchanged a knowing look.

'I told you he wouldn't be satisfied with just cutting a throat,' I said with an air of confidence. I followed the constable out of the yard and climbed into a waiting hansom cab. The driver urged the horse on, as we quickly made our way through the streets to the next murder scene in Mitre Square.

As we arrived, I found P.C. Edward Watkins standing guard at the south side of the square. Doctor George William Sequeira was standing by with a grim expression on his face, waiting for me to arrive.

'What do we have here, Watkins?' I asked the police constable.

'Another murder, sir. It's a nasty business, poor woman's been torn apart,' he replied, shaking his head in disgust.

I sighed, knowing that my prediction had come true. This was the work of the infamous Jack the Ripper. 'What do we know so far?' I asked, turning to Doctor Sequeira.

'Her throat has been brutally slashed, just like the other victims,' he stated. 'But there are also signs of mutilation. And it seems that the killer took a part of her body with him.'

I closed my eyes, feeling a sense of exhaustion and frustration wash over me. 'This is getting worse and worse,' I muttered.

At around 3 a.m., police constable Alfred Long whilst walking his beat along Goulston Street, found something laying in a stairwell of some of the tenements. On closer inspection, it turned out to be a piece of bloodstained cloth, and on the wall above it a message was written in chalk.

It read: THE JEWES ARE THE MEN THAT WILL NOT BE BLAMED FOR NOTHING.

Constable Long then informed us of the find, and very soon I arrived at the scene with a number of constables in tow. I ordered PC Long to make a copy of the message in his notebook, and it wasn't very long after that that a coach pulled up, and police commissioner Charles Warren stepped out. What have we here? Inspector Abberline he asked. I led the commissioner to the message on the wall, and he looked closely at the words. After a minute or two, he turned to me and said, Do you realize what trouble this message could cause if people saw the words written here inspector Abberline, it would cause more riots and anti Jewish demonstrations in the streets of London. We must remove this graffiti at once.

Then turning to one of the police officers, he ordered him to fetch a bucket and scrubbing brush and remove the offending message.

That day we found out that the piece of bloodstained cloth had been torn from the woman's apron in Mitre Square, and the killer must have used it to wipe the blood from his knife and hands as he made his escape.

We combed the streets, conducting interviews and asking for any information that could lead us to the killer. But as hard as we searched, Jack the Ripper seemed to elude us at every turn.

That very afternoon, I arrived at the mortuary to find out what wounds this maniac had inflicted upon the poor woman that now lay cold upon the slab of marble within this house of death. The smell of death and decay filled my nostrils as I made my way through the dimly lit halls. The atmosphere was heavy and somber, a stark contrast to the hustle and bustle of the busy streets outside.

As I entered the examination room, I found Doctor Frederick Brown working alone on the post mortem. He greeted me with a polite nod and a smile, beckoning me over to the table where the body of the victim lay. I could see that he had already begun his examination, the woman's lifeless body stripped of all dignity and laid bare for all to see.

'We have had a positive identification of the poor woman,' Doctor Brown informed me, his voice heavy with sorrow. 'Her name is Catherine Eddowes.'

I looked down at the woman's corpse, taking in her pale, lifeless face and the numerous wounds that now marred her body. This so-called 'Jack the Ripper' had truly gone to town on this poor creature. Her throat had been deeply slashed, just like his other victims, leaving a gruesome and gaping wound. But, as I soon found out, the brutality did not end there.

'When I was at the murder scene in Mitre Square,' Doctor Brown continued, 'the woman was laying with her head against a coal hole. Blood was oozing from her neck and pooling on the cobbles of the street.'

'Her abdomen had been cut with one long continuous slice from the breast bone right down to the vagina,' Doctor Brown went on, his voice now filled with disgust. 'Her intestines had been drawn out and placed upon her right shoulder, and were smeared with some feculent matter.'

I couldn't help but feel sickened as I heard the details of the victim's injuries. It was clear that the killer, whoever he may be, took great pleasure in inflicting this pain and suffering.

'Do you see these v-shaped cuts on her cheeks?'

Doctor Brown pointed to the woman's face, which now bore two deep and jagged gashes. 'It seems as though he also took the time to mutilate her face.'

I shook my head in disbelief. How could someone be capable of such depravity?

But the horrors did not end there. Doctor Brown continued to list off the numerous injuries and mutilations that adorned the woman's body. A piece of skin had been detached and placed between her body and left arm, her eyelids had been cut, and her right ear had been severed. And to top it all off, her left kidney had been removed and was nowhere to be found.

'The level of brutality and precision in these wounds is astounding,' I said, breaking the silence that had fallen over the room.

'I have never seen anything like it in all my years as a doctor,' Doctor Brown replied, wiping the blood from his hands with a cloth.

'How long would it have taken our murderer to inflict such wounds?' I asked, my mind reeling at the thought of the killer spending so much time with his victim.

'I should say at least five minutes,' Doctor Brown replied after a moment of contemplation. 'But I believe it is the work of one person.'

As I thanked the doctor for his time and left the mortuary, my mind was filled with the haunting image of the mutilated woman. It was clear that this killer was not just a common criminal, but a cold and calculated monster.

As I made my way back to the police station, my thoughts turned to the letter that had been received at the Central News Agency. In it, the sender had taken responsibility for the murder to come, and made mention of 'clipping the lady's ears.' The details matched perfectly with what I had just seen in the mortuary. It was clear that this was the work of the same killer.

But who was this madman? And how could one person be capable of such gruesome acts?

As I entered the police station, I knew that there was much work to be done. My team and I needed to gather as much information as possible, to track down this killer before he struck again.

Little did I know that the murders that took place in the autumn of 1888 would go down in history as one of the most elusive and infamous cases of all time. The identity of Jack the Ripper still remains a mystery to this day, and the horrors that he inflicted upon his victims still haunt the streets of London.

But for me, that afternoon at the mortuary will forever be ingrained in my memory, a reminder of the brutal and senseless violence that human beings are capable of.

25

Charles Allen Lechmere – from Beyond the Grave. The Bloody Cloth

My name is Charles Allen Lechmere, and I speak to you from beyond the grave. After I had killed the whore and mutilated her body, I was overcome with a sense of power and control. and the voices in my head stopped their screaming.

I tore some cloth from the whore's apron and quickly ran from the darkness of Mitre Square. Once I was in the streets that had gas lighting, I wiped the blood from my knife and hands with the cloth and placed it in my pocket. I knew I had to act fast and make my escape before anyone saw me.

I made my way through the deserted streets at a quick pace, my heart racing with adrenaline. I knew that time was of the essence, for I had to reach the safety of my mother's house before the authorities could catch wind of my gruesome deed. But as I turned down Goulston Street, I stopped in my tracks when I saw something written on the wall of the stairwell of one of the tenements in chalk.

'THE JEWES ARE NOT THE MEN THAT WILL BE BLAMED FOR NOTHING', it read.

It was an anti-Semitic message. I was not a Jew, and I wanted no part in this senseless hatred. But then a thought crossed my mind - what if I could use this to my advantage?

Without hesitation, I reached into my pocket and took out the bloody rag. If I left it under the graffiti, it would surely lead the people of London to once again blame the Jews and direct their anger towards them. I dropped the rag below the graffiti and continued my escape.

But my elation was short-lived. Not long before I reached my mother's house, I encountered five prostitutes in an alleyway. They blocked my path, and one of them spoke up in a seductive tone, 'Fancy a little excitement, luv?'

I ignored them and tried to pass, but another one spat in my direction and said, 'Yah know girls, I think e may be a lovea of boys - a queer.' They all burst into laughter, and I had to bite my lip to keep from lashing out at them.

'Ya never know, Liz,' one of them continued, 'maybe e's that Jack the Ripper bloke that the coppers are lookin for. Oh, but he's too puny to be a killer, said another, at which they all laughed corsley at me.

I turned and glared at them, my fists clenched in anger and frustration. But I knew I couldn't afford to blow my cover now. and I couldn't let their crude taunting get to me. Don't forget luv, cried one, if ever yah get tired of fuckin boys, and wanna real woman, just you ask for Lizzie Jackson. Once more they laughed at me as I turned my back.

Oh I'll remember your name alright Elizabeth Jackson, I thought to myself, and when we meet again you shall know me by a different name, and so will your friends.

Without a word, I continued down the alleyway, my mind racing with paranoia. What if they did suspect me of being the Ripper? What if they went to the police? No, I thought, I would bide my time before I dealt with those whore bitches. I still had work to do, and the next whore I would leave in such a state, that even the police doctors would be appalled at the site of her mutilated body. Jack the Ripper was about to go hunting the streets of Whitechapel once more, and this time it would be that whore bitch Mary Kelly.

26

George Lusk – from Beyond the Grave. From Hell

My name is George Lusk, and I speak to you from beyond the grave. It has been over a century since I walked the streets of Whitechapel, but my story is one that continues to haunt the people of London. I was the chairman of the Whitechapel vigilance committee in 1888, and I started it with one goal in mind - to catch the fiend who was walking the dark streets of Whitechapel, and murdering prostitutes.

At the time, the streets of Whitechapel were a dangerous place to be, especially for women. The notorious serial killer, known as Jack the Ripper, was on the loose and terrorizing the neighborhood.

The committee was formed to bridge the gap between the police and the community, as there was a growing sense of mistrust towards the authorities.

It was on the morning of October 16th, 1888, that everything changed. I received a cardboard box in the post, and upon opening it, I found it to contain a bloody kidney and a letter addressed to myself, written in red ink. The contents of the box were enough to make anyone's stomach turn. I was disgusted, and upon reading the letter, I knew that it was something that needed to be brought to the attention of the police.

I wasted no time, and immediately made my way to the local police station. The Sergeant at the desk was taken aback by my sudden and urgent appearance. I explained everything to him, and he left to confer with the inspector that was incharge of the investigation. After a few minutes, he returned and told me to follow him. I was led to the office of an inspector by the name of Abberline.

He greeted me with a nod and asked me to take a seat. I could see the exhaustion in his eyes, as if he had been working tirelessly for days. I took the box from under my arm and placed it on the table.

Inspector Abberline then opened it, and his expression changed from one of fatigue to shock.

He looked at the kidney, then took the letter from me. I could tell that he was deep in thought as he read it out loud, the words sending shivers down my spine.

'FROM HELL. MR. LUSK SOR. I SENT YOU HALF THE KIDNEY I TOOK FROM ONE WOMAN PRESARVED IT FOR YOU TOTHER PIECE I. FRIED. AND ATE. IT WAS VERY NISE. I MAY SEND YOU THE BLOODY KNIFE THAT TOOK IT OUT IF YOU ONLY WATE A WHIL LONGER. SIGNED CATCH ME IF YOU CAN MISHTER LUSK'.

Abberline sat with his hands steepled for some seconds before saying, 'Thanks, for bringing this letter to our attention, Mr. Lusk. You must know that we have had hundreds of letters, all reporting to be from the murderer. You may have seen some of them in the newspapers,' he paused, 'but I think that this letter may be from the maniac himself. Not only do we have a piece of kidney, which his last victim was found with a kidney removed, but the handwriting seems very similar to the 'Dear Boss' letter from last month.'

I couldn't believe what I was hearing. The fact that this letter may actually be from the killer sent chills down my spine. Abberline continued, 'The other thing is the deliberate spelling mistakes in this letter. It is as if he is trying to make us believe that he is uneducated.

However, if you take a look at the 'Dear Boss' letter, you will find that his spelling is almost perfect.'

I was stunned. It made sense and yet, it also didn't. Why would the killer deliberately misspell words?

Was he trying to throw off the police? Or was it some kind of game to him?

Abberline and I spent the next hour discussing the letter, analyzing every word and every mistake. We both came to the same conclusion - this could be our chance to catch the Whitechapel murderer.

Unfortunately, we were never able to catch Jack the Ripper. The letters continued to come in from 'Jack' and the killings continued. But even now, all these years later, people are still fascinated by the gruesome events of 1888. And for me, I will always be remembered as the man who received the infamous 'From Hell' letter.

My name is George Lusk, and even in death, I continue to speak about the horrors of that time. May my story serve as a lesson - a reminder that evil can lurk in the most unexpected of places, and that we must always be vigilant.

As for the Whitechapel vigilance committee, it disbanded not long after the events of 1888. But the memory of those brave men who tried to bring an end to the terror of Jack the Ripper will live on. And though the case remains unsolved, we will never forget those who lost their lives to the hands of a madman.

27

Charles Allen Lechmere – from Beyond the Grave. The Murder of Mary Jane Kelly

My name is Charles Allen Lechmere, and I speak to you from beyond the grave. My next victim was the whore Mary Jane Kelly. On the 9th November 1888, I made my way to the Ten Bells Pub for a drink. The streets of Whitechapel were dark and eerie, but I paid no mind. I was a regular at the pub and well-known among its patrons.

As I entered, the smell of ale and tobacco filled my nostrils. The pub was bustling with people, and I made my way to my usual seat in the corner, where I could observe the comings and goings without drawing too much attention to myself.

But on this night, as I sat sipping my first pint of beer, my eyes were drawn to the whore Mary Kelly. She was in the company of some men in the corner of the pub, a sly seductive smile on her lips. She was beautiful, with long fiery red hair and soft, inviting curves. But her profession made her undesirable to men like me, respectable men. I hated all whores, and it was my duty to rid the streets of them.

Kelly was obviously very drunk, stumbling as she made her way around the public bar, desperately trying to pick up a client. She came over to my corner, swaying slightly on her feet. 'Want a little bit of excitement?' she slurred, her voice thick with alcohol.

I looked at her with disdain, but played along. 'I may do,' I answered, enjoying the game.

'Well, I can take you to somewhere private,' she said, her eyes lighting up with a seductive gleam.

I raised an eyebrow in interest. 'I would like that.'

'Meet me outside in ten minutes, and I'll take you to my rooms,' she said, running her fingers through her hair.

'Okay,' I said, taking a sip of my beer. 'I have a little something we can share,' I added, showing her the bottle of gin I had asked the barman for. Her eyes lit up at the sight of it.

She returned to the other side of the bar, and I finished my drink, my mind already planning my next move. After a few minutes, I left the pub, making sure to slip unnoticed into the shadows.

Five minutes later, Kelly suddenly appeared, her eyes darting around nervously. Spotting me, she made her way over and took my arm, her voice low and husky as she said, 'Come with me, I shall take you to my room. I don't do business on the streets anymore because of this Jack the Ripper bloke.'

I let her lead me through the dark streets, my mind racing with excitement. We arrived at a small room in a building known as Miller's Court. She asked me to come in, but I pretended to hesitate. 'I must leave you for about half an hour, but I will return after that,' I said smoothly, giving her the bottle of gin with a knowing smile.

She smiled back, her eyes alight with anticipation. 'I can wait,' she said, her voice sultry. I shall lock the door, because you can never be sure who is roaming the streets these days. But upon your return you can always get in by reaching through that broken window and turning the key, don't be long, I shall await your return, she said with a smile.

I left and stood in the shadows for some minutes, looking in through the window, my heart racing with anticipation. In half an hour's time, Mary Jane Kelly would take her last breath. I couldn't wait to see the fear in her eyes as she realized that I was not the client she thought me to be. As soon as she had closed the door, she opened the bottle of gin and drank greedily from the bottle.

I made my way back to the pub, excitement bubbling inside of me. I was eager to see the effects of the laudanum, a potent opiate I had added to the bottle of gin. I knew it would relax her and make her drowsy, but hopefully not enough to render her unconscious. I wanted her to be awake, to feel everything. As I sat in the dimly lit pub, my thoughts were consumed with hatred. Hatred for the world and all its vices. But most of all, I hated Mary Jane Kelly.

She was a filthy whore, corrupting men left and right with her dirty, disease-ridden body. And tonight, I was going to put an end to her.

I had grown tired of seeing women like Kelly roam the streets, taking advantage of men and defiling themselves for a few coins. So, I took it upon myself to rid the world of this filth.

I sat for half an hour, sipping my ale and keeping a watchful eye on the door. I couldn't risk anyone recognizing me in the streets tonight. As I finished my drink, I quietly made my way out of the pub and into the dark streets of Whitechapel.

I knew she would be expecting me, and as I approached Miller's Court, I saw that she had prepared for my return. An old sheet was draped across the window of her room, a futile attempt to hide from the world.

I crept up to the window, peering inside. The room was dimly lit by the flickering fire, and I could see Kelly lying on her filthy bed, a half empty bottle of gin beside her. I tried the door, but it was locked from within. I smirked to myself.

Without hesitation, I moved to the broken window and reached in, turning the key in the door and making my way inside. The room was filled with the stench of alcohol and sweat, and I could feel my blood boiling.

With quiet steps, I made my way to the corner where I found a scarf. I approached the bed, standing over Kelly for a moment before she even realized I was there. And then, I struck.

Grabbing her by the neck, I pinned her down and shoved the scarf into her mouth. She fought against me, but I was too strong. She clawed at my hands, but it was no use. I hit her in the face, knocking her senseless onto the bed.

'Now, you filthy whore,' I hissed. 'Now, you will pay for all the filthy things you have done. Especially to my uncle Sid.'

Holding her down I drew my knife and stabbed her, a familiar feeling of pleasure washing over me. And then, in a frenzy, I began to mutilate her body.

I stabbed at her neck and her abdomen, relishing in every thrust. I cut her face, destroying her beauty and ensuring that no one would ever lay eyes on it again. I cut off her breasts, peeled the flesh from her bones, and removed her intestines and internal organs, scattering them around the room.

But I couldn't bring myself to stop. This was my mission, my duty to the world. To rid it of impure beings like Kelly.

After I had finished, I cleaned my knife and hands before looking out of the broken window once more. The darkness of Whitechapel greeted me, and I slipped into it, satisfied with my night's work.

28

Frederick Abberline – from Beyond the Grave. Senseless Murder

My name is Frederick Abberline and I speak to you from beyond the grave. It was on the morning of the 9th November 1888, that I was called to another crime scene. I had been working as a detective inspector for the Metropolitan Police in Whitechapel for several years now, but this particular case had thrown a shock throughout the entire city of London. It was now known as the infamous Jack the Ripper case, where several women had been brutally murdered and the killer was still on the loose.

As I sat in my office, still half asleep and nursing a hangover from the previous night's whiskey, I received a call from my superior Superintendent Thomas Arnold. He informed me that a new body had been found in Miller's court and requested my presence at the scene. I quickly ordered a hansom cab to take me to the crime scene.

Upon my arrival, I found my colleagues Inspector Beck, Superintendent Thomas Arnold, and Inspector Edmund Reid already there. The whole area was blocked off, preventing any members of the public from entering. It seemed that the crowds had gathered again, curious to see the latest victim of the Ripper. I made my way towards my fellow officers, dodging the reporters and journalists who were trying to get a glimpse of the crime scene.

Beck greeted me with a grim look on his face. 'We've had no luck with the bloodhounds this time, Abberline. It seems that the

Ripper has eluded us again.' I nodded, knowing all too well the frustration and helplessness we all felt. We had been hunting this killer for months now, but he always seemed one step ahead of us.

I walked over to the window and peered in. The room was small and cramped, with dirty furniture and a grimy window that barely let any light in. But what caught my attention was the sight before my eyes - a scene of slaughter. Blood and guts had been thrown about the room, staining the walls and floor. And in the corner, I could make out what was left of the poor woman, her body lying lifeless on the bed.

'Who found her?' I asked my comrades.

'She was found by the landlord's assistant around 10:45,' replied Superintendent Arnold. 'He had come to collect some weeks' rent arrears from the deceased, but when he received no answer at the door, he looked through the window and saw the body. He immediately summoned the police.'

'It's a horrible business, Inspector Abberline. A horrible business indeed,' added Superintendent Thomas Arnold, shaking his head.

At 1:30 p.m., Superintendent Arnold gave the order to break down the door. As we made our way into the room, the stench of blood, guts, and human excrement hit us like a brick wall.

The younger police officers, who were unused to such gruesome sights, stumbled out of the room and vomited. The sight and stench were too much for them to bear.

Inside, the atmosphere was oppressive. The room was hot and stuffy, and a fierce fire burned in the grate. It appeared that the Ripper had torn the poor woman's clothes from her and placed them on the fire to give himself better light to carry out his terrible deed. The stench was coming from the remains of the fire, where bits of flesh and clothing could still be seen burning.

As the lone police surgeon George Baxter Phillips examined the body, I couldn't help but feel a deep sense of despair. The Ripper had struck again, and this time, the brutality of the murder was unfathomable. The poor woman's body was barely recognizable, her organs spilled out onto the bed, and her throat was slit from ear to ear.

After the examination, two police photographs were taken of the body before it was then taken to the mortuary. As I stood in the room, still trying to make sense of the gruesome scene before me, I couldn't help but wonder why the Ripper was doing this. What twisted mind was capable of such atrocities?

Despite our best efforts, we were no closer to catching him than we were when he first appeared on the streets of Whitechapel.

It was a dreary November afternoon when I found myself at the morgue. I had grown all too familiar with the smell of death that lingered in this place, especially in the wake of the recent murders in Whitechapel. As I walked through the dimly lit hallways, I could feel a heavy weight settling on my shoulders, knowing that another innocent life had been brutally taken.

As I entered the examination room, I was met with the sight of two doctors, Thomas Bond and George Baxter Phillips, hunched over the body of the latest victim from Miller's Court. The body was that of a woman, her name now identified by the doctors as Mary Jane Kelly. I had not known her name until now, and I couldn't help but feel a pang of guilt for not being able to protect her and the other victims.

'Hello, Inspector Abberline,' Dr. Phillips greeted me, breaking me out of my thoughts. 'I suppose you are here to find out what we have found.'

I nodded, keeping my face neutral as I took in the gruesome scene before me. 'Yes, please tell me what you have uncovered.'

Dr. Bond motioned for me to come closer, and I reluctantly made my way to the examination table. The body lay there, completely mutilated and unrecognizable. I couldn't help but feel a surge of anger towards the maniac who had committed such heinous acts.

'As you can see, our murderer has removed the whole surface of the abdomen and thighs, and emptied out her vital organs,' Dr. Bond said solemnly. 'The contents of the abdomen were then thrown around the room.'

I fought back the urge to retch as I looked at the mess surrounding the table. It was evident that the killer had gone to great lengths to cause as much pain and suffering as possible.

'Her breasts have been cut off, and the arms have been mutilated by several jagged wounds,' Dr.

Phillips added, his voice shaking with emotion. 'The poor woman's face has also been hacked beyond recognition of the features.'

The details of the victim's injuries were enough to make one's blood run cold. I couldn't imagine the terror the poor woman must have felt in her last moments.

'Don't forget to mention the organs that were placed under her head,' Dr. Bond reminded his colleague, his voice laced with sadness. 'Her uterus, kidneys, and one breast were found there. The other breast was by her right foot, the liver between her feet, and the intestines by her right side. And let's not forget the spleen at her left.'

I couldn't believe the level of depravity that was on display. The killer had not only taken her life but had also desecrated her body in the most inhuman manner.

'The flaps of skin removed from her abdomen and thighs were laid on the table,' Dr. Phillips continued, his voice trembling with emotion. 'And her nose, cheeks, eyebrows, lips, and ears have been cut off as well.'

I felt my heart sink with every new detail that was being revealed to me. This was not just a murder, it was a brutal and savage act of violence.

'I think our killer kept the victim alive for as long as possible,' Dr. Bond spoke up again, his voice heavy with sadness. 'So she would feel the pain and suffer.'

I couldn't fathom why someone would do such a thing. What twisted mind could find pleasure in causing such agony to an innocent human being? I shook my head, unable to comprehend the depths of evil that existed in this world.

'What makes you think that she was still alive during the attacks?' I asked, wanting to understand the doctors' reasoning.

'Well, Inspector,' Dr. Bond began, 'as you will be aware, at all of the other murder scenes, there was very little blood around the bodies. This suggests that the victims were already dead when the killer inflicted the cuts and wounds upon their bodies.

However, at the scene of this poor woman's murder, there was a definite spray of blood.'

Dr. Phillips nodded in agreement, 'Yes, it covered the wall next to the bed. This shows that the victim was still alive during the brutal attacks.'

I couldn't believe what I was hearing. The killer had not only taken pleasure in murdering his victim, but had also taken joy in her suffering. The thought alone was enough to make me sick to my stomach.

I sighed, running a hand through my hair as I looked down at the lifeless body of the woman. Another victim, another senseless act of violence. I knew that solving these murders would not bring back the lives that had been taken, but it was my duty to find the culprit and bring him to justice.

As I exited the morgue and walked back into the cold and unwelcoming streets of Whitechapel, I couldn't help but feel a sense of hopelessness. The stench of death still lingered in the air, a constant reminder of the horrors that had taken place. But I knew that I had to keep going, keep searching for the answers that would put an end to these senseless killings. It was the only way to honor the memories of the victims and bring some semblance of peace to the people of Whitechapel.

29

Lechmere
– The Butcher of Whitechapel

My name is Charles Allen Lechmere, and I speak to you from beyond the grave. I have told you the story of how I became known as the infamous Jack the Ripper. But my killing spree didn't end in 1888, it had only just begun.

As the historians and coppers only credited me with a possible five victims, I sit here now to reveal the truth about the many others who fell victim to me in the shadows of the dark streets of London. I was a calculated and cunning killer, preying on the vulnerable women of the night.

My first two victims, the whore Polly Nichols and Black Martha Tabram, were just the beginning. As the city buzzed with the news of their gruesome deaths, I continued to hunt for more prey. It was during this time that my mother was living in Cable Street. Her cat's meat business had grown very profitable, and she had even rented a lock up under one of the railway arches nearby. It was a short walk from her home, but my stepfather's deteriorating health had left my mother with little time to run the business.

You see, my stepfather was suffering from senile dementia and could no longer be left alone. As the only son, I couldn't let my mother down in her time of need. Her cat's meat business was her only means of support, and I couldn't bear the thought of her struggling. So after finishing my last drop off for Pickford's, I would take my cart to the local knacker's yard to pick up some horse meat. I would then bring it back to the lock up and drop it off before returning to the Pickford's Depot.

Once I returned, I would rub down and feed my horses before walking back towards Cable Street. As I entered the lockup, and closed the door, I would cut and prepare the meat for my mother. She would then set out with a four wheeled hand cart to sell the meat the next day, while my aunt would sit with my stepfather for a few hours.

My aunt lived close by and had recently lost her husband, and was only to pleased to help out.

It was at this time that I set out to find the whores who had humiliated me and belittled me in the alleyway the night that I killed Catherine Eddowes. For days I searched the streets of Whitechapel with no results. Until on one rainy evening, I took shelter in a pub on Cable Street called The Horns and Horseshoe. I made my way to the bar and ordered a pint, and a double whisky to warm me up, and went to a corner seat and looked around.

The pub was fairly packed. The customers being working men of many trades, and sailors from the London Docks, and amongst these there were the whores trying their hardest to relieve the punters of their hard earned cash. They would make their way through the bar, sitting on men's laps, and pulling down their blouses to show some cleavage, and they had a quick eye for anyone who's wallet was fat with notes and coins. As I sipped my drink, my eyes roamed the bar, until suddenly I spotted that whore bitch Elizabeth Jackson sitting on a sailor's knee in the far corner of the bar. My heart raced and my fists clenched as I remembered that night in the alleyway.

I immediately put my flat cap upon my head, and pulled down the peak, so as not to be recognized by the bitch. I had to be careful, But I couldn't let her get away with what she did to me. I hated all whores, they were filthy, disease-ridden creatures who preyed on the vulnerable men of Whitechapel. And Elizabeth Jackson was the filthiest of them all.

Having no luck with the group of sailors she decided to try her luck elsewhere, and slowly made her way around the pub, working from table to table, until she reached mine. 'Allo ducks,' she said in her seductive way. Obviously she didn't recognize me from the night we met in the alleyway. 'Wanna a bit a fun luv, Lizzie will for fill ya every need.'

I just shook my head, and kept looking at my drink. No thanks love, perhaps another night I replied. Ok darlin, she replies, 'just yah remember to call on Lizzie Jackson when yah ready for a bit of excitement darlin, I'll take yah to eaven and back, just ya ask any of me regulars darlin.' With that, she moved on to her next potential client.

I found out from one of the regulars that the whore and her friends frequented this pub on most nights, and Elizabeth Jackson slept rough on most nights down near the docks. I finished my drink and left the pub, my mind racing as I thought about my next move.

I had to find a way to make that filth pay for what she did to me. I couldn't let her go free, not while I roamed the streets a wanted man. I went home, and started to plan my revenge.

The next few evenings were spent stalking Elizabeth Jackson. I followed her every move, watching as she charmed and manipulated men, just like she did to me. But this time, things were different. This time, I was in control.

∗∗∗

Over the next few days, I followed the whore, and soon found out the names of her fellow prostitutes. There names were Alice McKenzie, Frances Coles, and Ellen Walker. The other woman I couldn't find out her name, but she was known on the streets as dark Bessie.

During the times that I followed them, I made mental notes of the places they did business, and the pubs they went to. Coles rented a room in Whites Row, while McKenzie lived in a doss house on Wentworth Street. Elizabeth Jackson and dark Bessie both lived rough near the docks, taking shelter beneath a railway bridge, when business wasn't good.

I followed for a day or two longer, before I decided to take my revenge on the filthy whores. Coles and McKenzie I would deal with in the usual manner, a knife to the throat. Elizabeth Jackson, Ellen Walker, and dark Bessie, however, I had something special planned for them.

I spent the next few days making my plans. My Mother's lock up was just a few streets over from where the whores lived and worked. It was stocked with plenty of knives, saw's and butcher's tools for cutting up the horse meat, tools I would need for my plan.

Then I waited. I waited for each of the whores to make their usual rounds, and when they did, I struck.

30

Donald Swanson – from Beyond the Grave

My name is Donald Swanson, and I speak to you from beyond the grave. I shall now tell of some grizzly murders that took place in 1888 and 1889. Two of which seemed to bare a resemblance to some other murders that took place at the time. These murders had come to be known as the Whitechapel murders, and were being committed by a maniac who had become known as Jack the Ripper. As an inspector with the Scotland Yard during that time, I was tasked with solving these terrifying and brutal crimes.

It was on the 17th October 1888, that I was called to inspect a strange package that had been found in the basement of the new Scotland Yard building that was being constructed at 4 Whitehall Place.

Upon my arrival, I was shown what seemed to be the naked torso of a woman. It had been discovered by the workmen who were constructing the building. The body was mutilated beyond recognition, and the stench was unbearable. As I examined the torso, I was joined by surgeon Thomas Bond, who was also working on the case.

Together, we carefully inspected every inch of the torso. As Bond removed the cloth that had been wrapped around the body, we noticed the arms, legs, and head had been cleanly severed from the torso. Upon closer examination at the mortuary, Bond told me of a human right arm and shoulder, which had been washed up on the muddy shore of the River Thames at Pimlico on the 11th September. He had preserved it, and upon comparing it to the Whitehall torso, he concluded that they were a perfect match.

But with no clues at the scene and no birthmarks on the woman's remains, we had very little to go on. No one came forward to say that any relatives or friends had gone missing, so we couldn't even say who the poor woman was. But it resembled another case that had occurred in May and June of 1887.

During that time, the remains of a woman's body were found in the River Thames near Rainham. Workers had encountered a bundle containing the torso of a woman. Throughout May and June of that year, various other parts of the same body were found, with the exception of the head and upper chest. Again, we had no leads, and the woman was marked down as unknown on the police records.

As more evidence came to light, we were determined to catch the culprit responsible for these heinous acts. But with no witnesses and no solid leads, our investigation was at a standstill. In the months following the gruesome discovery of the torso in Whitehall, the city of London was filled with fear and suspicion. No one knew who the killer was, or when he would strike again. We had been working tirelessly to find any leads or clues that could help us catch the killer, but to no avail.

Every day, we would go to the crime scene and analyze every detail, hoping to find something that could lead us to the killer. But as the week's went by, the case began to grow cold and the killer seemed to have disappeared into thin air. It was as if they had vanished from the face of the earth.

Then one day, after seven long months of peace, another torso was found in the Thames, It was a female torso and it was found on the 4th of June 1889. We knew that we had to work fast before more innocent lives were taken.

As we continued our investigation, more and more body parts were discovered. A left leg was found at Battersea, the lower part of the abdomen at Horsleydown, the liver near Nine Elms. The upper part of the body was found in Battersea Park, and the neck and shoulders were discovered on the Battersea shore. A right foot and leg were found at Wandsworth, a left leg and foot at

Limehouse, and a left arm and hand at Bankside. The buttocks and pelvis were found at the Battersea shore, and the right thigh was found at Chelsea Embankment.

It was horrifying to think of all these body parts scattered across different locations. It was as if the killer was taunting us, leaving a trail of clues for us to follow. But no matter how hard we searched, we could not find the missing pieces of the puzzle - the heads of the victims.

Despite the lack of leads and clues, we were able to identify the second victim. She was a Whitechapel prostitute by the name of Elizabeth Jackson. But even with this information, we were no closer to catching the killer. We had no suspects, no motives, and no solid evidence to work with.

In the months following the gruesome discovery of the torso in Whitehall, the city of London was filled with fear and suspicion. No one knew who the killer was or when they would strike again. We had been working tirelessly to find any leads or clues that could help us catch the killer, but to no avail.

Months went by, and the case went cold once again. It seemed like the killer had vanished into the shadows and we were left with nothing but a pile of body parts and unanswered questions. The city of London was living in constant fear, wondering if they would be the next victim to be found dismembered and scattered across the city.

On a wet morning on the 17th July 1889, I received a call from PC Walter Andrews who was patrolling his beat in the dark and dingy streets of Whitechapel. He had made a grisly discovery - a woman lying in a narrow alleyway between Whitechapel Road and Wentworth Street.

According to PC Andrews, the woman had her throat cut and there were some abdominal injuries inflicted upon her.

I immediately rushed to the scene, collecting my equipment and grabbing my raincoat along the way. As I made my way through the rain-soaked streets, I couldn't help but feel a sense of dread.

The infamous Jack the Ripper had been terrorizing this area for months, and every discovery of a murdered woman made my heart race with fear and frustration.

When I arrived at the scene, PC Andrews' description was confirmed. The woman, who appeared to be a prostitute, had indeed been brutally attacked. I asked the police doctor who was already examining the body for his initial findings. 'It looks like the Rippers work Donald,' he said, turning to me. 'The wounds bare his trademark.

The throat has been cut deeply, right down to the vertebral column. There are some wounds to the lower abdomen, but there is no deliberate mutilation that I can see. Which tells me either our killer was disturbed in the act, or this isn't the work of the maniac, and is someone else's handy work.'

I thanked the doctor and quickly surveyed the scene. The alleyway was dark and secluded, making it a perfect spot for a gruesome murder. It seemed like the victim had been killed where she was found, as there were no drag marks or signs of a struggle. PC Andrews had tried to cover her with his coat to protect her from the rain, but it was obvious that she had been dead for a while.

When the body was eventually removed, we noticed something strange. The pavement beneath the woman was dry, despite the rain that had been pouring down for a while. This led us to believe that the woman had been murdered sometime before 12:45 a.m., when the rain had started. We also found some footprints in the muddy ground nearby, but they were too faint to be of any use.

The body was taken to the mortuary and after a thorough examination, it was identified as Alice McKenzie, a known prostitute in the area. Her death further confirmed our suspicions that Jack the Ripper was targeting prostitutes in Whitechapel again. But despite the growing number of murders, we had no leads and no real suspect.

The verdict of Alice McKenzie's death at the coroner's court was death by person or persons unknown. It was a frustrating and disheartening outcome for us, as it seemed like this killer would never be brought to justice. The streets of Whitechapel were filled with fear and the residents were demanding answers and protection from the police.

The rain continued to pour as the days went by and the hunt for Jack the Ripper continued. But even as we patrolled the streets, questioning suspects and following leads, we couldn't shake off the sense of desperation and helplessness. It seemed like this elusive killer would always be one step ahead of us.

It was the morning of September 10th, 1889, and I was just settling into my office at the Whitechapel Police Station when a commotion broke out. I was informed by one of my officers that another woman's torso had been found, just two months after the brutal murder of Alice McKenzie.

I quickly made my way to Pinchin Street, where the torso was reportedly found. As I arrived, I saw PC William Pennett, who had been the one to make the discovery, standing in front of a dark railway arch. I approached him and asked, 'What have we here, constable?'

'It is the dismembered body of a woman, sir,' PC Pennett replied.

'How did you come upon the poor woman, constable?' I asked, hoping to gather any information that could lead us to the killer.

'Well, sir, I was walking my beat and at 5:15 I heard the church clock strike the quarter hour. So, I checked my watch and lit my torch. I always use a torch at that time of the morning sir, as there is very little light on the street,' PC Pennett explained.

I nodded, urging him to continue.

'As I made my way along Pinchin Street sir, I started to search all the dark corners, including the railway arches. I always make a point of checking them to make sure no one is sleeping rough or up to any monkey business with the local prostitutes,' he continued, using a term for illegal activity that I was all too familiar with.

'I see,' I replied, knowing all too well the seedy activities that took place in the shadows of Whitechapel at night.

'And, if I may say so sir, I always check the railway arches. And I can positively say that when I passed through here about three quarters of an hour before, there was no sign of the woman's remains,' PC Pennett added, his voice filled with confusion and concern.

'Thank you, constable. Has a doctor been sent for?' I asked, turning my attention to the task at hand.

'Yes, sir. As soon as I found the body, I blew my whistle for assistance. And a few minutes later, PC Jones and PC Johnson arrived on the scene. I took the liberty of sending PC Johnson for the doctor and PC Jones for a hand cart,' PC Pennett replied, visibly relieved to have more experienced officers to assist him.

'You have done well, constable,' I said, patting him on the shoulder before walking over to the railway arch to examine the remains.

A few moments later, Dr. Baxter arrived at the scene, and with his expertise, we were able to determine that the cuts on the torso were about a day old. This information was vital, as it meant that the killer had most likely held onto the body for a period of time before disposing of it in this dark corner of the railway arch.

After the gruesome finding of the woman's torso in Pinchin Street, our murderer went quiet for about six months. The community was still living in fear, not knowing when this madman would strike again. We worked tirelessly to find any leads or clues that could lead us to the killer.

But on the 13th of February, 1891, our worst fears came true once more. At 2:15 a.m., PC Ernest Thompson was walking his beat along Swallow Gardens when he came across a woman lying under a dark and grimy railway arch. Her throat had been cut, but she was still clinging onto life. Upon seeing the body, PC Thompson heard somebody running away from the scene. He didn't give chase, as police protocol stated that he must stay with the body until help arrived.

Thompson, a newly appointed constable, made the discovery on what was the first solo beat of his career. Quickly, he blew his whistle for assistance, and within moments, three more police officers from the local area arrived. One of them was sent to inform me, and within fifteen minutes, I was at the scene. PC Thompson had stayed with the woman until an ambulance arrived to take her to the hospital, but unfortunately, she passed away from her wounds before she arrived.

I thanked PC Thompson for staying with the body and quickly asked him for his report. We searched the area for any clues but found nothing sir. I immediately returned to the police station and sent out some of my officers to gather information about the unfortunate woman. We soon learned her name was Frances Coles, a known prostitute of the Whitechapel area. Her partner, James Sadler, was a ship's fireman who had a reputation for being gruff and violent, often turning to alcohol for solace.

After further investigation, we discovered that Coles and Sadler had been seen arguing on the night of her murder. This immediately raised suspicion, and we brought Sadler in for questioning on the same day. But rumors started circulating that he could be Jack the Ripper, and we couldn't ignore it. We delved deeper into his background, but investigations showed that he was away at sea during the time of the previous murders in 1888.

Despite this, we couldn't let him go without a thorough interrogation. Sadler's demeanor was tense, and he seemed to have something to hide. On the 16th of February, we made the decision to charge Sadler with Coles' murder. He was taken to trial, but his defense was led by the powerful seaman's union, and with no concrete evidence, he was acquitted of the crime.

As the last recorded victim of the Whitechapel murders, the city finally found some semblance of peace. But I couldn't shake the feeling that Jack the Ripper may have killed many more, and we would never know the extent of his heinous actions.

Years went by, and the case remained unsolved. The streets of Whitechapel returned to their bustling ways, but the scars of the murders still lingered.

Every time I walked by the railway arch where we found Frances Coles, memories of that night flooded back. I had been so sure that Sadler was the killer, but I was wrong.

It wasn't until many years later that a journalist, Robert Anderson, came to me with a theory. He believed that Jack the Ripper was a man named Francis Tumblety, an American doctor who had a grudge against women after a failed romantic relationship. But even with this new information, I couldn't help but wonder if we would ever know the true identity of the Ripper.

It has been over a hundred years since the Whitechapel murders, but the mystery still lives on. The city has changed so much, and the memories of that dark time are fading. But for me, the events of those terrible months will forever be ingrained in my mind.

31

Charles Lechmere
– from Beyond the Grave

My name is Charles Allen Lechmere, and I speak to you from beyond the grave. I shall now tell of the so called Thames Torso mysteries, and my involvement in them. After making my plans to murder the whore Elizabeth Jackson and her friends, I thought to change my method of murder. I remembered reading a newspaper article back in May of 1887, about a strange package that had been discovered washed up on the shore. It contained the torso of a woman. Throughout the month, more body parts were found along the river. No one was ever arrested for the crime, and the case went cold.

Remembering the report, I thought to myself, what if I were to copy the Rainham mystery. It would direct the police away from my crimes as Jack the Ripper, and lead them on a false trail. Half of the focus would be taken from me, when they went in search of the so called Thames Torso murderer. Yes it could work, I thought to myself with smile. As I have told in my story so far, I had already been stalking the whore Elizabeth Jackson and her friends. I knew now which streets they worked, the pubs they went to, and where each one of them lived. So after a few days, I made my first move. I found Dark Bessie standing on a street corner not very far from Cable Street in the pouring rain. I walked down the pavement, pretending to not notice the whore. Ellow ducks, she said as I passed by. Fancy a good time, only cost ya fourpence luv. I stopped and looked at the bitch for some seconds, before saying. You look wet and cold my dear. That I am, she answers. Cold wet and bleedin ungry. If you come with me I can give you food, and shelter from this horrible weather, then once you have eaten, maybe you would like to share this with me I said, showing her the bottle of Gin I had already laced with Laudanum. At the sight of the Gin, Dark Bessie's eyes lit up.

And taking her by the arm, I led her through the wet streets, and into my mother's lockup. Making sure nobody had seen me, I locked the door. Once inside I opened the Gin, and passed it to the whore. She drank greedily from the bottle, and it wasn't long before she collapsed upon the floor. Taking my knife, I quickly cut her throat, then set about dismembering her body, with knife, saw, and meat cleaver. Digging a hole in the earth floor in a dark corner, I threw in the head, and a good layer of quick lime, then covering it with earth I firmed it with my foot. Turning to the other body parts, I quickly loaded them into the four wheeled cart, and covering it with sacking, I wheeled it out into the wet streets of Whitechapel. I knew where I would dump the torso of Dark Bessie, for I wanted to leave a little surprise for the coppers. As I made my way through Whitechapel, not one person looked my way, for I was dressed in my usual work clothes, and most people were used to seeing me with my cart at this time of night. I was even cocky enough to stop and chat to one of the local bobby's, who was patrolling the streets. It gave me a rush of adrenaline to think if only he knew what I had under the sacking. But after we had chatted for a few minutes, I said goodnight, and continued on my way, chuckling to myself. Very soon I reached the place were they were building the new Scotland yard in Whitehall. Making sure all was quiet, I lifted the sack that contained the torso, and dumped it in the basement of the new building, just for jolly, I said to myself with a smile. I then made my way to the new tower bridge that was being constructed over the Thames, and using one of the many wooden builders jetty's, I dumped the other body parts into the river where all the other rubbish of London was thrown.

Elizabeth Jackson was the easiest of my victim's, all I had to do was wait in the shadows near the Horns and Horseshoe pub, and wait for the whore bitch to come out. It was a cold dark night, and a thin drizzle was falling. After some waiting, I saw the bitch come out of the pub holding a sailors arm. I ducked back into the shadows of my hiding place, and looked on, as she tried her hardest to get business. But the sailors soon left, and the whore made her way down the cold wet street towards me. Pulling my flat cap low, I made my way to a lampost and stood beneath it's dim light. Upon seeing me, the whore quickly made her way towards me, asking if I fancied a bit of fun. I accepted her offer, and told her that I knew of a dry place where we could go to get out of the rain, and if she wanted she could spend the night there safe and dry from the cold and rain. She took the bait, and taking my arm, I led her down the road, where she met the same fate as that whore Dark Bessie. I dumped her dismembered body into the river, and let the tide do the rest.

Ellen Walker met the same fate three months later, and after I had dispatched her, the voices in my head suddenly stopped their screaming, and I knew that I had full filled my mission for God. After that I was able to return to a fairly peaceful life style. I would go to work each day, and return to Elizabeth and my children every evening. Every night we would sit by the fire, and I would read to my beautiful wife.

My mother lost my stepfather in late 1889, and I carried on helping her with her cat's meat business until her death in 1902. She had saved a tidy sum of money whilst running her business, and left me two hundred pounds in her will. I then left Pickford's, and opened up a little shop on the Whitechapel Road, selling everything from fresh vegetables, to meat and tobacco. I became well respected for the service I gave, and my prices, which I always kept low.

I lived happily for the remainder of my years, never moving from London's East End. After my killing spree ended in 1889, the case of the Whitechapel murders was soon closed, and London took a sigh of relief. I still have no regrets or remorse for my actions against the whores of the East End, and only wish that I could have killed more.

My life came to an end on the 23rd December 1920, and I was layed to rest in Tower Hamlets cemetery. And although you may have never heard of my name before, and the name of Charles Allen Lechmere has been forgotten, I know that even after death, I shall be remembered for a thousand years or more, by my other name, yours truly, JACK THE RIPPER.

*Available worldwide from Amazon
and all good bookstores*

Michael Terence Publishing

www.mtp.agency

mtp.agency

@mtp_agency